Mansa Musa and Timbuktu

A Captivating Guide to the Emperor of the Mali Empire and a Major City for Trade in Medieval West Africa

© Copyright 2021

All Rights Reserved. No part of this book may be reproduced in any form without permission in writing from the author. Reviewers may quote brief passages in reviews.

Disclaimer: No part of this publication may be reproduced or transmitted in any form or by any means, mechanical or electronic, including photocopying or recording, or by any information storage and retrieval system, or transmitted by email without permission in writing from the publisher.

While all attempts have been made to verify the information provided in this publication, neither the author nor the publisher assumes any responsibility for errors, omissions or contrary interpretations of the subject matter herein.

This book is for entertainment purposes only. The views expressed are those of the author alone, and should not be taken as expert instruction or commands. The reader is responsible for his or her own actions.

Adherence to all applicable laws and regulations, including international, federal, state and local laws governing professional licensing, business practices, advertising and all other aspects of doing business in the US, Canada, UK or any other jurisdiction is the sole responsibility of the purchaser or reader.

Neither the author nor the publisher assumes any responsibility or liability whatsoever on the behalf of the purchaser or reader of these materials. Any perceived slight of any individual or organization is purely unintentional.

Free Bonus from Captivating History (Available for a Limited time)

Hi History Lovers!

Now you have a chance to join our exclusive history list so you can get your first history ebook for free as well as discounts and a potential to get more history books for free! Simply visit the link below to join.

Captivatinghistory.com/ebook

Also, make sure to follow us on Facebook, Twitter and Youtube by searching for Captivating History.

Table of Contents

PART 1: MANSA MUSA 1
    INTRODUCTION: A GOLDEN EMPEROR IN A GOLDEN AGE......... 2
    CHAPTER 1 - THE FOREFATHERS OF MANSA MUSA 6
    CHAPTER 2 - MANSA MUSA COMES TO THE THRONE............... 18
    CHAPTER 3 - MANSA MUSA GETS READY FOR THE HAJJ 24
    CHAPTER 4 - AND THEY'RE OFF! 31
    CHAPTER 5 - MANSA MUSA MAKES HIS MOVE............................. 37
    CHAPTER 6 - IN THE LAND OF EGYPT 44
    CHAPTER 7 - MANSA RESUMES HIS PILGRIMAGE........................ 53
    CHAPTER 8 - HEADING BACK HOME 59
    CHAPTER 9 - RETURN TO THE CAPITAL... 66
    CHAPTER 10 - MALI AFTER MANSA MUSA 71
    CONCLUSION: THE LEGACY OF AN EMPIRE 86
PART 2: TIMBUKTU.. 90
    INTRODUCTION 91
    CHAPTER 1 - TIMBUKTU'S CREATION AND ITS FIRST
    PEOPLE (BEGINNING-13TH CENTURY) 93
    CHAPTER 2 - THE MALI EMPIRE (AROUND 1200-1255) 102
    CHAPTER 3 - THE SUBSEQUENT MONARCHS OF THE MALI
    EMPIRE (1255-1312) 108

CHAPTER 4 – MANSA MUSA (1312-1337) 116
CHAPTER 5 – THE MALI EMPIRE AFTER MANSA MUSA (1337-1360) 136
CHAPTER 6 – THE CONTINUATION OF THE FAGA LAYE LINEAGE AND THE DOWNFALL OF THE MALI EMPIRE (1360-1389) 142
CHAPTER 7 – THE FINAL MANSAS OF THE MALI EMPIRE AND ITS COLLAPSE (1389-THE BEGINNING OF THE 17TH CENTURY) 150
CHAPTER 8 – THE SONGHAI EMPIRE (1464-1591) 161
CHAPTER 9 – THE DOWNFALL OF THE SONGHAI EMPIRE, THE MOROCCAN OCCUPATION, AND THE FRENCH INVASION (1591-1900) 167
CHAPTER 10 – TIMBUKTU IN THE 20TH AND 21ST CENTURIES (1900-2021) 173
CONCLUSION 181
HERE'S ANOTHER BOOK BY CAPTIVATING HISTORY THAT YOU MIGHT LIKE 183
FREE BONUS FROM CAPTIVATING HISTORY (AVAILABLE FOR A LIMITED TIME) 184
BIBLIOGRAPHY 185

Part 1: Mansa Musa

A Captivating Guide to the Emperor of the Islamic Mali Empire in West Africa and How He Developed Timbuktu into a Major Center for Trade

Introduction: A Golden Emperor in a Golden Age

His proud and regal face stares out at us from old medieval maps, donning a golden crown and holding a golden globe in the palm of his hand. There is just something very special about the West African monarch named Mansa Musa, who lived during the High Middle Ages. The Catalan Atlas, which features the illustrated image of Mansa Musa, was actually drawn up in 1375, several decades after Mansa Musa had already passed. Contrary to its name, the book isn't actually an atlas, as it just contains one map.

The fact that Mansa Musa was still remembered all those years later—remembered enough to put his face on a map—indicates just how stunning a figure Mansa Musa really was. The Catalan Atlas, composed by a Spanish, more specifically Majorcan, cartographer named Abraham Cresques, was a standard and mainstay for medieval explorers. Cresques had been hired by Prince John of Aragon to create a map of the known world.

This was, of course, over one hundred years before the American continents were known (excluding the Vikings' jaunt to Canada), so the "known world" of those days, at least among Europeans, primarily consisted of Europe, Asia, and Africa. It was on the portion of the Catalan Atlas that designated West Africa that we find the intriguing illustration of Mansa Musa, who is seated on a throne with a nugget of pure gold in his raised hand.

All of the subsequent intrepid explorers who saw the noble visage of Mansa Musa staring back at them as they did their best to use the Catalan Atlas to navigate through unknown lands and waters must have wondered just who this great African king was. Although there is still much that has yet to be uncovered about Mansa Musa's life, fortunately, through the piecing together of historical records, Mali lore, and archaeological finds, that once puzzling picture has become a little clearer.

Mansa Musa ruled from his throne in his capital city of Niani, which literally sat right on top of a gold mine. In those days, Mali is believed to have had some of the largest gold deposits in the world, and Mansa Musa's successful stewardship of these resources—according to modern estimates—most likely made him the richest man who ever lived. Mansa Musa is, in fact, estimated to have had a net worth that would be very near four hundred billion dollars in today's US currency.

Just to put that into perspective, the current richest human being on the planet (at least as of this writing) is a man named Elon Musk. Musk has a net worth of almost 200 billion dollars. It is indeed rather incredible to think that even with all of the resources and commercial expertise of the modern world today, our current richest figure is worth only roughly half of what this little-known Malian emperor—Mansa Musa—had at his disposal in the Middle Ages.

"Disposal" is perhaps the best word to describe Mansa Musa's monetary capacity since he was so rich, he was able to dispose of his riches at a moment's notice and in any way he pleased. Although much of his life is shrouded in mystery, one of the most memorable moments of his existence occurred when he visited Cairo while on the hajj and managed to singlehandedly crash the gold markets! He did this through purchases as well as blatant generosity. Just imagine this West African ruler arriving in Cairo, Egypt, and handing out gold bars to random people on the street as if it were nothing!

Mansa Musa unloaded so much gold in Egypt that it sunk the value of this precious metal in the Egyptian economy, and the repercussions lasted over a decade after Mansa Musa's departure. After all, gold is valuable because of its scarcity. So, if everyone you know suddenly has a pile of gold in their lap, this rare metal is not worth quite as much anymore.

Mali had more gold than anywhere else in the world at this time, and the sudden unloading of a large quantity of it in Egypt kicked off a spate of hyperinflation that put the Egyptian merchants and financial brokers to shame. It was this exploit more than anything else that sent shockwaves through the Middle East, across the Mediterranean, and on into Europe. Soon, many heads of state around the world were whispering about the mysterious Mali emperor who had so much gold that he did not quite know what to do with it.

But after returning from his hajj, Mansa Musa did make some very wise investments. In 1324, while Musa was still abroad during his hajj, his top general, Sagamandia, had managed to annex two major trading cities—Gao and Timbuktu—to the realm. Mansa Musa used all of the resources at his disposal to make these two West African metropolises stand out as not only centers of immense commerce and trade but also of learning.

He hired top-of-the-line architects to build mosques, schools, and government buildings, some of which still stand to this day. Subsequent explorers, such as the famed Muslim scholar Ibn Battuta, later visited these sites and marveled at their construction. The (Islamic school) of Sankore, which would ultimately become the University of Sankore, would draw thousands of dedicated students and boasted a library that housed countless scholastic texts and valuable manuscripts.

Mansa Musa not only wanted to enrich his empire with material wealth but also with a legacy of learning and education. It was these efforts that would leave the most lasting imprint on his empire. Long after the gold was gone and the salt mines may have dried up, these storied centers of knowledge remain fixed in the sands of the desert regions of Gao and Timbuktu, just as they are fixed in the sands of time.

In all, Mansa Musa ruled the Mali Empire for twenty-five years, and by all accounts, he was entirely beloved by his people. According to Arab historian Ibn Kathir, he was a dashing, charismatic, and charming figure. Ibn Kathir described Mansa Musa as being "a young, handsome man, who had 24 kings under his authority." Under Mansa Musa's rule, these subordinate kings would serve as governors for a sprawling empire that took up much of West Africa. And as the Catalan Atlas can attest, the Mali Empire was West Africa.

Mansa Musa reigned over a vast empire. He wore a golden crown, carried golden weapons, sat on a grand throne, and held firm to a golden staff. It is really no wonder that he was known as the golden emperor. It truly was a golden age for Mali and, by extension, a golden age for the whole world.

Chapter 1 – The Forefathers of Mansa Musa

"I have the mohawk. I don't wanna be disrespectful to the Mohican Indians but there is a tribe in Africa called the Mandinka warriors. They're in the west coast of Africa in the country of Mali. I was reading National Geographic Magazine back in 1977, and I saw the warrior standing there with his spear and his beads around his neck and whatnot, and the stuff on his ankles. That was what gave me the idea, I said, 'Wow, let me bring respect to them,' so basically what I wear is called a Mandinka cut."

-Mr. T

From the very beginning of recorded history, the African continent has always been held as a place of mystery and wonder. The prospect of obtaining wondrous wealth in the form of Africa's sub-Saharan gold deposits has long brought various parties from far and wide. As early as 400 CE, local African kingdoms found themselves in a power struggle over who would control this wealth. And by around 800 CE, it was the Kingdoms of Ghana, Songhai (also sometimes spelled as "Songhay"), and Mali, in particular, that began to rule the region.

Of these kingdoms, Ghana began to dominate early on, with the Kingdom of Mali as a client state. When the Kingdom of Ghana went into decline, Mali became the dominant player in the region. Mali then reached empire status in the 900s, and it would become its most powerful during the 1200s, by which time it had supplanted the Kingdom of Ghana entirely. During Mali's reign as the greatest empire of West Africa, one of the most prominent rulers was a man named Sundiata Keita (also sometimes called Mari Diata, Mari Djata, or Mari Jata).

Most of what we know of Sundiata Keita comes down to us through oral history, which has been passed down from one generation to the next. The purveyors of this oral history belonged to a specialized group of Mali storytellers called the griots. It was the griots who were charged with committing important historical events to memory and also typically served as advisors to their rulers.

According to griot lore, Sundiata was the son of the princess Sogolon Conde and King Nare Maghann Konate. The griot lore records that both Sundiata and his mother, Sogolon Conde, were cruelly mocked and ridiculed by their peers. Sogolon was apparently the object of ridicule because of her appearance. She was actually described as being an "ugly hunchback" with huge eyeballs that bulged out of her head.

The griot lore passed down to us also contends that Sogolon was a powerful sorceress who could shapeshift into animal forms. As the story goes, when she grew weary of being a hunchbacked woman, she would transform into a humpbacked buffalo of all things. Another version of the tale says that Sogolon actually became cursed after she killed her sister in a fit of rage. At any rate, if Sogolon was supposedly so horrible, frightening, and downright atrocious, one might naturally wonder why did King Nare Maghann Konate marry her?

The reason was quite simple. Nare Maghann Konate's own soothsayers foretold that if he married "an ugly woman," she would give birth to a powerful king. In following this lead, Nare Maghann Konate set about searching for the "ugly woman" that his diviners had foretold. He was later convinced that it was none other than Sogolon Conde, as she fit that description.

Having such a reputation was certainly not flattering, to say the least. But Sogolon Conde, despite her rough physical appearance, seemed to have some level of at least cautious respect from the masses. She was, after all, said to be a powerful sorceress. Having said that, most did not really want to get on her bad side lest she cast some sort of spell on them. But if Nare Maghann Konate expected her to birth a child who would jump up out of the cradle as someone clearly destined for future greatness, he would be sorely disappointed.

The pregnancy was apparently a difficult one, and it is said to have lasted an unusually long amount of time. Some griot lore, in fact, speaks of Sogolon for being pregnant for over a year! Whatever the case may be, when Sogolon finally gave birth to Sundiata, it was clear that he would have a challenging existence, as Sundiata was seemingly dealt a difficult hand in life due to a childhood illness that left him "crippled" and unable to walk without assistance.

There was no such thing as political correctness in those days, and according to griot oral testimony, Sundiata was mercilessly teased over his disability. In fact, it seemed that the people came to believe that Sundiata deserved the affliction due to his mother's own dark magic, and they assumed the child was essentially cursed. The idea that those with deformities and disabilities are cursed is, sadly, a long-running theme in many West African cultures. To this very day, you can find villages in Mali where children suffering from birth defects such as a cleft lip are routinely mocked and/or shunned by those who feel it was the hands of fate (or a witch) who cleft their lip rather than mere genetic happenstance. It goes without saying that such harsh treatment would be devastating for any child wishing to grow up and do something productive with their life, let alone someday become a great leader.

And as it pertains to Sundiata, the griots are quite clear that Sundiata's neighbors really did believe that there was something terribly wrong with him. In fact, they not only believed it but also resented him for it. This feeling of resentment was then reinforced after Sogolon gave birth to Sundiata's little sister, Kolonkan, and his little brother, Bori, who both apparently turned out healthy and robust while Sundiata remained severely challenged. To resent a child for birth defects he had no control over seems rather despicable, especially from today's viewpoint, but this is apparently what happened.

Nevertheless, Sundiata used the mockery that he was bombarded with to encourage himself, and one day, out of sheer determination, he suddenly rose to his feet and forced himself to walk. The villagers viewed this happenstance as nothing short of a miraculous sign. From this day forward, rather than being mocked, Sundiata became a well-respected member of the community. For a time, it seemed that the hardship of Sundiata's past was behind him.

But when his father, Nare Maghann Konate, abruptly passed away, the young man's life would take another sharp turn. After the passing of his father, Sundiata's political opponents began to plot and scheme for the throne. Soon, he and his family were once again the targets of malicious abuse. Things got so bad that Sogolon Conde took Sundiata and his siblings and fled the country. Sogolon basically grabbed her kids, had them carry whatever they could on their backs, and ran.

This led to an exodus through many regions of what was then the Ghana Empire. In their quest for safe asylum, they eventually made their way to a place called Mema, whose king finally granted them the safety and security that they sought. The king of Mema is said to have become quite close to Sundiata during his stay, and he came to see great potential in the young prince. Eventually, the king decided to offer Sundiata a job. He made Sundiata a royal official in his realm. And while Sundiata was working in this capacity for the king of Mema, word was sent that the Mandinka people of Mali had been defeated by the Kingdom of Sosso. Emissaries were sent, hoping that Sundiata, whom some had previously prophesied would be a great leader, would come and rescue them.

Belief is indeed a powerful thing. Sundiata's deceased father had died still believing the promise of his soothsayers that his son, Sundiata, was destined for great things. In the society that Sundiata came from, the proclamations of those perceived to be prophets were considered sacrosanct and beyond dispute. Thus, Sundiata's fellow countrymen began to believe in the fate that had been prophesied for Sundiata as well. It is indeed rather ironic that the man who many rejected and was driven out of his own country would be beseeched in such a manner when the chips were down, but according to griot lore, this is precisely what happened.

Sundiata could have simply ignored those who called for his aid and lived quite happily in the courts of the king of Mema. By this time, his mother, Sogolon, had perished. It is not entirely clear how she died, but it seems to have been of natural causes during their stay at the Mema court. At any rate, her passing potentially could have had the effect of erasing any last connection her adult son may have had to his ancestral homeland. Why should he rush in and help those who had been so cruel to him and his family? Was the pull of his prophesized greatness really enough to make him return to such a hateful place? But Sundiata was not one to hold petty grievances, and ancestral fealty ran deep within him. Feeling the call of destiny, he agreed to liberate those he still considered to be his people.

Sundiata was able to cobble together an army courtesy of the Mema king, and with these troops, he launched his liberation campaign of Mali. These troops then hooked up with the remaining independent warlords of Mali to root out the Sosso conquerors. The Sosso were ultimately destroyed at the Battle of Kirina, an engagement that took place in the Koulikoro Region of Mali, and as a result, Sundiata became the first emperor or mansa of the Mali Empire. The actual battle itself is believed to have taken place sometime around the year 1230 CE.

Although the details are rather scant, the Battle of Kirina was said to have been a cataclysmic event in which two powerful armies relentlessly smashed into each other. It is said that during this conflict, Sundiata managed to kill Sumanguru Kante, the Sosso king himself, with a poison-tipped arrow. Some versions of the story, however, claim that after Sundiata discovered that Sumanguru's spirit animal was a "rooster," he fixed a "cock's spur" to his arrow and fired it at Sumanguru.

Legend tells that the brave Sundiata attached the bird's clawed foot to the end of an arrow, pulled back his bow, and sent the improvised missile hurling toward Sumanguru. The arrow itself did not do much damage. All this clawed arrow did was nick the warlord, but supposedly, it knocked down the magical protective shield that had heretofore kept him from harm.

According to this version of the story, Sumanguru, who was an accomplished sorcerer, was virtually invulnerable in battle until Sundiata managed to discover this one chink in his spiritual armor. After this, it is suggested that Sumanguru was either killed or was otherwise somehow defeated (some versions suggest he was even magically turned to stone).

Yes, griot lore insists that both sides made great use of magic and witchcraft against their enemy. Sundiata was supposedly the son of a sorceress, so it would have only seemed fitting for such dark arts to have been used. Such things are, no doubt, hard for a modern reader to believe, but the mention of wizardry and witchcraft serves as a good demonstration of what the belief systems were in those days. This was, of course, before Islam became the religion of the land or at least of the ruling classes. Prior to Islam, most people in the region practiced ancestral shamanism.

At any rate, once the battle had been won, and both Sumanguru's castle and his "magic tower" were burned down, the victorious Sundiata made his capital at Niani, a strategic location fixed between modern-day Mali's border with Guinea. His empire would come to dominate almost all of West Africa. Sundiata's armies easily conquered the territory of what had been the old Ghana Empire, as well as added additional territory in what is today modern Senegal, Gambia, and Guinea Bissau.

The Mali Empire would come to control all of the important trade routes, which stretched from the rain forests to the south all the way to the Saharan deserts of North Africa. This allowed the leaders of Mali to control the gold trade as it was taken from the south to the north. Camels laden with gold traveling back and forth through the Mali Empire to places far and wide would soon become a common occurrence.

The interesting thing about how Mansa Sundiata handled his empire is that he chose to run the large tracts of the territory he gained as a federation. Rather than having top-heavy centralized control, he allowed each region to have its own local administrator who would handle local affairs, even though each administrator reported to the emperor (or the mansa) as the ultimate authority.

The Mali Empire also established what was known as the "Great Gbara Assembly," which was a form of parliament that placed a check on the emperor lest he overstep his bounds. It was rather forward-thinking of the Mali Empire to have such a system of checks and balances in place. Most kings and queens of the Middle

Ages ruled through "might makes right," whereas the Mali mansas had to make sure that their actions lined up with the Great Gbara Assembly.

The mansa was powerful for sure, but thanks to the Great Gbara Assembly, they were still held accountable for their actions all the same. The Great Gbara Assembly even had the power to remove the emperor if need be, and it was up to the assembly to designate the successor of the previous mansa. As it pertains to the man who became Mansa Sundiata, he successfully reigned within the bounds of this system for some twenty-five years.

Although it is not entirely clear what ultimately befell Sundiata, griot lore seems to indicate that he was the victim of a tragic accident. One version of events insists that he fell into a river, but another speaks of him accidentally being hit by an arrow—a poison arrow, in fact. Could it have been the wicked sorcerer king Sumanguru whom Sundiata had previously struck down, exacting his final revenge from beyond the grave? It certainly makes for a good story to tell around the campfire. But no one, not even those wise Mali heralds, the griots, seems to really know for sure.

But whatever may have happened, after his passing, Mansa Sundiata was ultimately succeeded by his son Uli (sometimes spelled as Ali or Wali). Mansa Uli was known as a powerful, successful ruler who expanded his reach all the way to the important commercial hub of Timbuktu. It is important to note that he did not annex Timbuktu outright (this would happen later), but he did make Timbuktu a part of the general Mali orbit.

He is also notable for converting to Islam and being the first mansa to undergo the hajj, a religious pilgrimage to Mecca, the holy city of Islam. It is recorded that he made his pilgrimage to Saudi Arabia during the time when a certain sultan named Baybars (or Baibars) reigned in Egypt, and Uli made his presence known when passing through Baybars's land. Mansa Uli's reign would last until the year 1270.

The next person to be selected as the mansa of Mali was Uli's brother, Wati. Mansa Wati would prove to be far less successful than his predecessors and would only remain in power for four years. It was after Mansa Wati's short rule that control of the Mali Empire fell upon the shoulders of another of Sundiata's descendants, this time, an adopted son named Khalifa. But Khalifa, who had a penchant for randomly shooting people with arrows (this was apparently a hobby of his), was quickly proven unfit to rule.

Cruel, insane, and tyrannical are the best adjectives to describe Khalifa, and it wasn't long before Khalifa was removed from power. The next man chosen for the job of mansa by the Great Gbara Assembly was Sundiata's grandson Abu Bakr (or Abubakari). It seems that Abu Bakr I was more or less a stooge for the elites, and he is thought to have been a kind of "puppet ruler" put in place by the assembly. Abu Bakr I would run the empire for twelve years before he was replaced in 1285 by a man named Sakura.

Of all the mansas so far, Sakura has one of the most unique stories, as he was apparently a former slave. Some sources also state that he was a military commander of some sort. Such transitions are not uncommon in African civilizations, and even former slaves often found opportunities to rise through the ranks. In fact, one of the most famous African slaves to rise to prominence is documented in none other than the Bible, although it must be noted that not all of the tales of the Old Testament have been historically validated. Regardless, if one considers the Bible, Prophet Joseph, who was enslaved in Egypt, later become one of the pharaoh's top commanders.

At any rate, Sakura—the former slave turned military leader—staged a successful coup that removed Abu Bakr I from power. Even though his seizure of power was illegal, he proved to be such a good leader that the political powers that be allowed him to remain mansa. He was indeed a steady hand at the helm, and under his leadership, the borders of the Mali Empire began to stretch eastward to the region of Gao, a region that would later be officially annexed under Mansa Musa.

Outside forces, however, would intervene, and Sakura's rein would come to an end in 1300 when he was murdered while returning home from Mecca. Traveling across the Sahara Desert was certainly not easy to begin with, and it wasn't uncommon for Bedouin bandits to make it even harder. Sakura's body was recovered, however, and it is recorded that Sakura was buried with full honor, befitting of a great Mali emperor. After Sakura, the next leader put forth by the assembly as mansa was a man named Gao, who was one of Kolonkan's sons. Kolonkan, if you don't remember, was Sundiata Keita's younger sister.

Mansa Gao's reign was another brief one, of which very little is recorded. After his reign came to an end, the power then passed to his son, Mohammad ibn Goa, in 1305 (although some sources state the year as being 1307). Mansa Mohammad was succeeded by a nephew of Sundiata, Abu Bakr (or Abubakri) II. Abu Bakr II is an intriguing individual because, according to legend, he actually sent a large expedition—large as in some two hundred ships—across the Atlantic in order to see what was on the other side.

This voyage allegedly occurred nearly two centuries before Christopher Columbus tried the same feat. According to tradition, of these two hundred ships that were sent out, only one returned. But the stories that this one returned vessel conveyed were so wonderous that Abu Bakr immediately prepared for a follow-up mission in which he himself would take part. This time, he went all out and prepared a fleet of two thousand ships, an armada that he would personally lead. Just before he left, however, he made sure Musa (also sometimes known as Kankan Musa) was named as his successor.

As the story goes, Abu Bakr II never found his way back. As the Mali ruler was thought to be lost for all time, Musa became the new leader (or mansa) of the empire, thus becoming Mansa Musa. The story of how Mansa Musa came to the throne is perhaps hard to believe. But as fanciful as it all might sound, it was a narrative that Mansa Musa himself repeated. An Arab scholar by the name of Al Umari actually recorded the words of Mansa Musa as he recalled this very sequence of events.

Mansa Musa allegedly explained:

The ruler who preceded me did not believe that it was impossible to reach the extremity of the ocean that encircles the earth, and wanted to reach that [the extremity] and obstinately persisted in the design. So he equipped two hundred boats full of men, like many others full of gold, water and victuals [food] sufficient enough for several years. He ordered the chief not to return until they had reached the extremity of the ocean, or if they had exhausted the provisions and the water. They set out. Their absence extended over a long period, and, at last, only one boat returned. On our questioning, the captain said: "Prince, we have navigated for a long time, until we saw in the midst of the ocean as if a big river was flowing violently. My boat was the last one; others were ahead of me. As soon as any of them reached this place, it drowned in the whirlpool and never came out. I sailed backwards to escape this current." But the Sultan would not believe him. He ordered two thousand boats to be equipped for him and for his men, and one thousand more for water and victuals. Then he conferred on me the regency during his absence, and departed with his men on the ocean trip, never to return nor to give a sign of life.

If this legend is true, one must wonder what actually happened to these Mali voyagers. Were they sucked up in a whirlpool? Prior to Columbus finding the New World and proving the nature of our round globe, many ordinary people actually believed that sailing across the Atlantic too far would cause one to fall right off the edge of the planet!

Whatever may have happened to Abu Bakr and his men, they were certainly brave enough to chart a course for the unknown. And the story doesn't end there because there are some who claim that these Mali explorers—at least those who didn't get sucked up in a whirlpool—actually made it all the way to at least one of the American continents.

Although its currently nothing more than pure conjecture, fueled by various anecdotal threads, some historians, such as Ivan Van Sertima, who was an expert on African history, have theorized that it might have been possible that these wayward explorers from Mali set up a colony in what's now known as modern-day Brazil.

One odd anomaly that seems to give credence to the notion of pre-Columbian contact with and travel to the Americas is the fact that archaeologists have long been baffled by discoveries of purely American produce being found in Old World archaeological sites where they shouldn't be. Just take the so-called "nicotine" mummies as a good example of this strange occurrence. In Egypt, mummies have been discovered that have remnants of nicotine on their person. As funny as the idea of smoking mummies might sound, the crazy thing is tobacco originated from the Americas. And according to the official narrative, no one in the Old World had tobacco until after Christopher Columbus. Yet, the nicotine mummies and other archaeological sites seem to defy this logic with their deposits of American goods that date back to pre-Columbian times.

However, critics are sure to assert that the nicotine may have found its way to the mummies through other more prosaic means, such as by way of an archaeologist or two who smoked heavily at a dig site and thereby contaminated the mummies. At any rate, whatever the case may be, it was due to the failure of Abu Bakr II to return from his epic trip across the Atlantic that Mansa Musa came to the imperial throne.

Chapter 2 – Mansa Musa Comes to the Throne

"And has the story of Musa come to you? When he saw fire, he said to his family: Stop, for surely I see a fire, haply I may bring to you therefrom a live coal or find a guidance at the fire. So when he came to it, a voice was uttered: Oh Musa! Surely I am your Lord, therefore put off our shoes; surely you are in the sacred valley, Tuwa. And I have chosen you, so listen to what is revealed. Surely I am Allah, there is no god but I, therefore serve me and keep up prayer for remembrance. Surely the hour is coming—I am about to make it manifest—so that every soul may be rewarded as it strives."

-Surah Taha 20: 9-15 (The Quran)

It is said that the Mali Empire, at its greatest extent, stretched from the Atlantic Ocean all the way to Lake Chad. This is a big chunk of western and part of central Africa. With it came great resources but also great responsibility. Mansa Musa's imperial leadership of the Mali Empire is said to have begun around the year 1312. For it was in this year that Mansa Musa was installed inside the imperial palace at the Mali capital of Niani, where he ruled alongside his queen and wife, Inari Kunate.

In the Mali Empire, it was common for the mansa to have a main wife, such as Inari Kunate, who would be considered the queen, along with additional wives who did not share that distinction. Not too much is known about Mansa Musa's royal bride Inari Kunate other than the fact that she eventually bore him a son by the name of Maghan. Mansa Maghan's later rule after his father's death is equally obscure, especially since it is basically just a footnote compared to his father's legacy. Some sources say that Mansa Maghan ruled for just a few years before he died.

At any rate, as it pertains to Mansa Musa, it was from his palace in Niani—the capital city of Mali—that the great mansa oversaw all the happenings of his realm. Here, he could be seen seated on a "grand seat of ebony, flanked by elephant tusks" as his court ministers kept him abreast of all of the latest developments. When the emperor sat on his grand throne, he was always flanked by his imperial retinue.

The interesting thing about the way the court system of the Mali Empire worked was the fact that it made use of an official "spokesman" who spoke on behalf of the emperor. The emperor himself was never directly spoken to. Any inquiries were always given to his intermediary, who then personally presented them to the mansa. The mansa then gave his response to the intermediary spokesman, who repeated it back to those who had inquired in the first place.

It's admittedly not the most efficient means of communicating with a sovereign, but it served the purpose of keeping the mansa's position as one that was especially revered and distinct. Another sign that those in an audience with the emperor were dealing with someone of authority was the fact that no one was allowed to wear sandals in his presence. This meant that those gathered around the mansa had to be barefoot at all times. Being in the presence of the mansa was considered so sacred, in fact, that even sneezing was barred! Yes, it was actually forbidden to sneeze in the presence of the mansa of Mali, and if the ruler himself happened to get a case of the sniffles, it was customary for all who were present to beat their chest as if they themselves were the ones with the cold. By displaying complete solidarity with their sovereign, the people showed that if their leader suffered, they suffered as well.

Mansa Musa was also always surrounded by a bodyguard unit, which was composed of his own personal slaves. Yes, Mansa Musa had slaves, but it is important to note that slavery in his realm and in many other parts of Africa was much different than how it came to be practiced in other parts of the world. In Mali, slaves, although subject to their owners, were not usually cruelly treated or discriminated against, and they were often given important tasks to fulfill at court, such as being the mansa's personal spokesman or as a griot, the historians of the court.

To be clear, the concept of owning another human being is wrong in all of its forms. But the nature of slavery in Mali was also clearly different than how it would later manifest in the trans-Atlantic slave trade or even the Arab slave trade. Both Europeans and Arabs tended to dehumanize their slaves, whereas indigenous slavery in West Africa was viewed as more of a temporary social class distinction. Having said that, slaves had a much greater chance of rising above their lowly station, as can be seen in the case of one of Mali's most renowned emperors, Mansa Sakura. Despite his former status of being a slave, Mansa Sakura rose to the top rung of Malian society. As long as he performed as an able and competent leader, which he apparently did, no one had any qualms with his previous condition.

It is said that the Mali Empire, in fact, had an official "prohibition" on any mistreatment of both enemy combatants or slaves for any reason. This does not mean that slaves were never mistreated; on some occasions, they most likely were. There are always mean and cruel people in the world who desire to treat others badly if they are given the opportunity. But the official stance of the kingdom was to treat slaves in what was deemed to be a fair manner.

One of the first edicts of import issued by Mansa Musa occurred during his first year on the throne when he decreed that Islam would be the Mali Empire's state religion. Prior to the determination to make Mali a Muslim empire, most of the people believed in African ancestral beliefs, but with Mansa Musa's order, Islam would become the religious standard of the land.

This doesn't mean that people abandoned their prior religious beliefs overnight. In fact, many kept practicing their native traditions even after this ordinance went out. Mansa Musa himself made it clear that although Islam was considered the official state religion, he would more or less tolerate other beliefs in his kingdom. And he certainly wasn't going to force anyone to unwillingly become a Muslim if they did not wish to do so. Had he tried, it no doubt would have sparked a rebellion among the lower classes, as they especially clung to their ancestral religion.

Mansa Musa was a shrewd enough ruler to know that nothing good would have come from such forced conversion. In allowing his subjects to retain their beliefs, he also showed a bit of latent superstition of his own. For Mansa Musa, through his observations, had come to the conclusion that the gold mines controlled by those who still practiced ancestral beliefs produced more gold than those who had converted to Islam.

Certainly, there must have been a rational explanation for this. Mansa Musa himself hit upon it in a later offhand remark that was recorded for posterity when he said something to the effect of "free people are more productive than those under duress." But whatever the case may be, Mansa Musa also took it as a sign that the gold mines under pagan administration were best left with their traditional mode of religion lest he somehow jinx the cash flow of the kingdom.

Many of the locals actually believed that a snake god was the force behind the gold deposits, and they routinely made the worship of this deity a centerpiece to their mining operations. Some sources even suggest that human sacrifice might have been carried out in the past in order to please the spirits. It is said that the gold miners in Mali were convinced that digging up gold was literally a matter of life and death in which both the living and the deceased took part.

But despite many in the lower classes sticking to more traditional beliefs, the upper classes embraced Islam as being the proper religious standard-bearer of the realm. Islam was seen as a vehicle to the upper crust of society. Converting the empire to Islam was also important for relations with Mali's neighbors in northern Africa, especially Morocco, since they too had long ago found their way into the house of Islam. Mali was now a member of the Muslim world, and its trade of commerce and culture would only benefit as a result.

Arab traders were, of course, a major part of the trading network in Africa, and since Mali's conversion, they felt more or less right at home in the Muslim Mali Empire. After making Islam the official religion of the empire, Mansa Musa furthered the Islamization of his realm by building several mosques, many with impressive minarets that reached the sky. From these houses of worship, the faithful would hear the call for prayer. Bearing testament to their solid architecture, some of these mosques are still in use to this very day.

But as great as his personal faith was while at home, since Mansa Musa was a Muslim, he was required to make the traditional hajj, or pilgrimage, to the holy city of Mecca in modern-day Saudi Arabia. Making a pilgrimage to Mecca is one of the Five Pillars of Islam, which all Muslims are meant to fulfill. The other pillars, simply put, are faith, prayer, worship, fasting, and alms-giving. So, if one is a dedicated Muslim, there is just no way of getting around the obligation of the hajj. No matter how far they may be from this centerpiece of Islam, all of the Muslim faithful are expected to reach Mecca at some point in their lifetime, that is, as long as they are able to make the arduous journey. And Mansa Musa's own personal journey would create an epic odyssey like no other.

Chapter 3 – Mansa Musa Gets Ready for the Hajj

"During the past eleven days here in the Muslim world, I have eaten from the same plate, drunk from the same glass and slept on the same rug—while praying to the same God—with fellow Muslims whose eyes were the bluest of the blue, whose hair was the blondest of blond, and whose skin was the whitest of white. And in the words and in the deeds of the white Muslims, I felt the same sincerity that I felt among the black African Muslims of Nigeria, Sudan and Ghana."

-Malcolm X

The hajj is a trip that all faithful Muslims are required to make at least once in their lifetime if they are able to. No matter where they live, those who have dedicated themselves to the hajj must make their way to the holy city of Mecca in Saudi Arabia. Since the Muslim faithful gather in this one spot from all corners of the Earth, the term "mecca" has become synonymous with the concept of an ultimate "gathering place" of enthusiasts. Just imagine being at a comic or science fiction convention, for example, and the comic-book-reading fan next to you suddenly exclaims, "By Jove! This is a real mecca for comic book fans!" Well, my friends, it is the very nature of the hajj, which drew people to this one city, that has caused the name of Mecca itself to become a descriptive term for a gathering place.

Those who successfully complete this journey are given the honorary title of being a hajji. For Mansa Musa, his journey would be an epic one that would take him through the deserts of North Africa, into Egypt, and then on into Saudi Arabia. He would cover over nine thousand miles, and the journey itself would take over a year to complete. There are a few alternating tales as to what inspired Mansa Musa to journey to Mecca when he did. One of the more intriguing narratives actually makes the claim that Mansa Musa "accidentally" killed his own mother, Nana Gongo (sometimes also called Kankou or Kanku).

According to this version of Mansa Musa lore, her death was apparently the result of some kind of freak accident, and Mansa Musa was horrified at what had happened. As intriguing as this happenstance seems to be, the traditional sources are strangely quiet as to just what kind of "accident" may have befallen Mansa Musa's mother. If this event really did occur, it would seem that Musa's family was somehow plagued with all kinds of bad luck. His ancestor Sundiata, after all, is also believed to have perished from an accidental death.

At any rate, in his grief, Musa tried to make amends by giving an excessive amount of alms to the poor. But when he still felt guilty about the whole ordeal, he turned to an Islamic cleric for advice. The cleric advised Mansa Musa that he should head off to Mecca and "seek sanctuary with the Prophet" so that he could request him to "intervene on his behalf with Allah."

Some other versions of the story indicate that his soothsayers simply gave him a random day on the calendar with which to begin his journey. According to West African historian David C. Conrad, the diviners, without much rhyme or reason, "told Mansa Musa he should wait until a Saturday that would fall on the 12th day of the month. This meant that he had to wait nine months before he could leave—which he did."

At any rate, he became motivated to go. In order to prepare for the trip, Mansa Musa went all out as far as provisions were concerned. He collected goods from all over the Mali Empire, and he also gathered up the best teachers and scholars that he could find to accompany him on the journey. In the end, Mansa Musa's retinue would consist of some sixty thousand subjects, with twelve thousand of them said to be members of Mansa's imperial court. He also took his wife, royal Queen Inari Kunate, with him, although their son, Maghan, stayed behind to function as the acting mansa in his father's absence.

Others who undertook the perilous journey of the hajj often had to risk their own lives traveling treacherous roads on which bandits preyed upon travelers. But Mansa Musa, with a veritable army surrounding him (eight thousand men in the group were soldiers), did not have to worry so much about banditry. All the bandits could do was watch with envy as Mansa Musa's camels carted some twenty-four thousand pounds of gold. Yes, Mansa Musa practically took a whole storehouse of gold with him.

In fact, Mansa Musa had so much gold that even his servants who accompanied the grand entourage of Mansa Musa's caravan are said to have each had a staff of solid gold in their possession. It must have broken a Bedouin's heart to see such great treasures passing through the desert and being completely unable to plunder it! Considering the great wealth of both gold and advisors that Mansa Musa brought with him, many have since speculated that Mansa Musa was seeking to turn his trip into a diplomatic one, although he was, of course, still going for spiritual reasons as well.

It only makes sense if you think about it. Since Mansa Musa was required by Islamic law to make the hajj to Mecca, he might as well develop strong diplomatic ties along the way. Places like Morocco, Libya, Egypt, and Saudi Arabia would have been important regional players that one should establish political ties with.

It was a big mission, but Mansa Musa didn't forget his responsibilities at home while he was away. As mentioned above, he left his son Maghan in charge, and if he were to fail to return, which had happened when Musa's predecessor, Abu Bakr II, failed to return all those years ago, his son would automatically take over the empire.

With all of these important matters of state squared away, it is said that Mansa Musa left around October, right at the end of the harvest season in the Mali Empire. The day of the mansa's departure was marked as one of celebration, in which all of the citizens took part. According to official lore, people gathered from all corners of the Mali Empire to see the emperor off. There were great speeches made in the emperor's honor, songs were sung, dances were danced, and sacrificial animals were placed upon the altar—all in preparation for the emperor's departure from the land.

Priests and holy men were also much sought after to bless the path of Mansa Musa's journey. It is important to note that although Mansa Musa himself was a Muslim, he, at least at this point in time, heartily embraced all of the various religious strains of his empire. And it is said that all modes of religious sentiment were on display on the day of his departure and that all were utilized in an effort to bless his trip. Considering the fact that some of his predecessors, such as the ill-fated slave-turned-king Mansa Sakura, did not return when they undertook their hajj, Mansa Musa no doubt probably figured he could use all of the blessings he could get.

The oral historians of the Mali Empire, the griots, recorded a rather strange event that allegedly occurred right before the emperor departed from the capital city of Niani. According to them, Mansa Musa requested four birds. Just four regular birds that you typically see singing and chattering away in the overhanging trees. Once these birds were acquired, the mansa then instructed his attendants to kill the birds and cut them up into pieces. Mansa Musa had the chopped-up bird bits scattered over the four hills of Niani. Most today would not enjoy the sight of dismembered birds, but Mansa Musa apparently took his inspiration from the Quran, which speaks of the ancient patriarch Abraham doing much the same thing, placing the dead remains of four birds on four hills.

As Surah 2:260 (The Cow) vividly describes, "And when Ibrahim [Abraham] said: My Lord! Show me how thou givest life to the dead, He [Allah] said: What! And do you not believe? He [Abraham] said: Yes, but that my heart may be at ease. He [Allah] said: Then take four of the birds, then train them to follow you, then place on every mountain a part of them, then call them, they will come to you flying; and know that Allah is Mighty, Wise."

According to the Quran, God (or Allah) then resurrected the birds and had them come flying back to Abraham as a sign. Mansa Musa repeated this practice himself before leaving Niani, and according to legend, he called the birds back to him just as Abraham had done. To the surprise of those assembled, the birds returned to him but not in physical form. Instead, those gathered were shocked to see what looked like birds of pure light flying toward the emperor. They then witnessed "a halo of light too strong for the naked eye" surround their king.

Such things might be a bit too difficult for a modern reader to believe, but the griots attest that it actually happened. And what happens next is even stranger, especially as the griots recorded it from Mansa Musa's own testimony. The emperor claimed that right after the halo of light surrounded him, everything suddenly came to a stop. Mansa Musa allegedly witnessed all of his subjects—every single one of the thousands gathered around him that day—suddenly freeze in place. Even the animals stood completely stock still and motionless.

It was as if someone had suddenly hit the pause button, with everyone standing like lifeless statues. According to Musa, it was as if time had come to a grinding halt for everyone but him. It is said that during this strange supernatural interval, Mansa Musa immediately came to the conclusion that this work was the product of divine intervention, and the great king fell to the ground to humble himself, absolutely certain that he was in the presence of God. Mansa Musa claimed that he was then visited by an angel who spoke to him briefly before he "commanded the birds to return."

The birds that had been chopped to bits miraculously reformed themselves, then joined the halo of light and took off over the horizon. According to Mansa Musa, it was after this feat that the angel vanished, and as if someone had suddenly pressed the play button, life and motion returned to all those around him. To his shock, his subjects and the animals came back to life as if nothing had happened—all of them completely unaware of the missing time they experienced in which they were in a state of suspended animation.

Mansa Musa stared in wonder, lost in the thought that all of those around him had been frozen in time but were completely unaware that it had happened in the first place. Mansa Musa thought to himself, "Where did the souls go during this common sleep?" If this event happened—and admittedly, that's a big if—Mansa Musa was apparently the only one who even knew it had occurred.

If such a thing was alleged by anyone other than the emperor, no one would have believed them. But since the words of their sovereign were considered sacrosanct, when he informed them of this bizarre occurrence, his subjects took it quite seriously, Although the griots were apparently unable to witness it in real time since they too were frozen in place during the event, they took down the words of their king and recorded his account in their oral testimony.

Mansa Musa's journey to Mecca would be full of all kinds of surprises and unexpected events. In Muslim tradition, the journey to Mecca is very much just as important as the arrival. It's a period of reflection and discovery in which the traveler can become more in tune with themselves and their relationship with the divine. Even for a great ruler like Mansa Musa, who had a large company of subjects accompany him, the journey was still an intensely personal one. And, according to the story of Mansa Musa's vision of the revived birds, which had the thousands of people around him suddenly freeze in suspended animation, God supposedly found a way to speak to Musa on a personal level, distinctly tailored just for him and his experience. Then again, if you choose not to believe in the possibility of the supernatural, such visionary experiences could be chalked up to being a combination of dreams or outright hallucination brought on by the heat. Although Mansa Musa and his followers had yet to traverse the vast desert, which is known to bring about mirages, standing out in the heat with no protection would have been enough to perhaps make one a little more prone to hallucinations. Heat stroke, after all, is a very real phenomenon, and its debilitating effects are widely known. But, of course, seeing a sandy mirage that looks like water rather than a sand dune is one thing; seeing thousands of your followers suddenly look like they are doing the mannequin challenge (an internet trend in which folks suddenly freeze in their tracks like mannequins) is another!

At any rate, after all of these festivities and supposed supernatural occurrences came to their conclusion, it is said that Mansa Musa "mounted his black stallion" before signaling to his retinue that he was ready to depart. Then, at his orders, the caravan's "red and yellow flags unfurled," his entourage began to move, and his long journey to Mecca began.

Chapter 4 – And They're Off!

"Their women are of surpassing beauty, and are shown more respect than the men. These people are Muslims, punctilious in observing the hours of prayer, studying the books of law, and memorizing the Koran. Yet their women show no bashfulness before men and do not veil themselves, though they are assiduous in attending prayers. Any man who wishes to marry one of them may do so, but they do not travel with their husbands, and, even if one desire to do so, her family would not allow her to go."

-Ibn Battuta

The emperor's entourage left the seat of the Mali Empire—the city of Niani—and headed east to the city of Mema. This was the same fabled city that Mansa Musa's ancestor, Mansa Sundiata, had sought refuge in when he was exiled from his kingdom. It was the great king of Mema who took the exiled prince in and saw to his needs, allowing Sundiata to gather his strength so that he could one day return in glorious triumph and found what would become the Mali Empire.

Mansa Musa knew this story all too well, thanks to the loyal griots who repeated the legend on a routine basis. Having said that, Mansa Musa most have stood in wonder as he gazed out at Mema's cityscape and pondered how far his empire had come. His forebearers were driven out of the land, but now, he, their descendant, was the master of a mighty domain that stretched from the Atlantic coast in the west all the way to Lake Chad in the central African Sahel.

At any rate, the emperor was a man on a mission, and he could not stay long. After a brief stop in Mema, the emperor led his entourage to the city of Walata (or Oualata), which borders the southernmost extremity of the Sahara Desert. This was a place of intense heat and dryness. There was a sense of barren desolation in this land, interspersed every so often with the rare sight of one or two palm trees. Mansa Musa and his followers would trek some five hundred miles through this desert as they continued to journey on toward their ultimate goal of Mecca.

Even though the emperor was moving away from the center of his empire, he had trustworthy couriers who continually traveled back and forth between him and his capital. It was the messengers' job to deliver important updates and also send official responses back from the emperor. The emperor and his caravan were, for all intents and purposes, a mobile government in itself. In fact, the emperor would assemble his own council on a daily basis in which status reports were given and directives were issued to all those present.

The life of this mobile kingdom went on, and as with any large gathering of people such as this, issues would arise. The mansa's subjects who were with him could get sick or even die while en route, and they would need to be attended to. Funerals most certainly occurred while on the road, and it was required that the mansa's people were given a proper burial, as it was demanded by tradition.

During their journey, the emperor's subjects were by no means idle, and they contributed to various needed tasks, such as fixing worn-out gear, fashioning new clothing, or going to a local market to replenish the reserves of grain and rice. As one can see, everyone had something to do during this long journey. The mansa's encampment also found time to make merry and have fun. It was a common occurrence at the end of a workweek for the emperor to host festivities right there in the desert, during which his best musicians played instruments such as "ten-stringed harps" and beat their drums as singers sang, dancers danced, and griots told stories of the bygone past.

If any random wayfarer in the Sahara saw this spectacle—if they could even believe it wasn't a mirage that they saw emerge in the middle of the desert—they must have been truly amazed at what they bore witness to. But none of these festivities could quite compare to the absolute bonanza that took place to commemorate the emperor's birth. Yes, life went on like it always did while the mansa and his entourage journeyed to Mecca, and when his birthday came to pass during his time in the desert, it was most certainly commemorated like it always would have been.

The emperor's birthday arrived just as his mobile kingdom reached the borders of Gourara. Mansa Musa and his inner court met with Gourara's governor and other important officials. In celebration of the event, fifty head of cattle were slaughtered, and plenty of rice was dished up. Interestingly, the horns of the cattle that were a part of the feast are said to have been dried out and given special preservation techniques, after which the hollowed-out horns had precious stones, herbal ingredients, and even pieces of Quran scripture stuffed inside of them. These were used as charms and as talismans to ward off evil. This was indeed a mixture of ancestral religion with aspects of Islam attached to it. The Quran itself, in fact, would object against such use since Muslim teaching bans the use of idols or talismans of any kind. But like many people around the world who end up mixing a mainstream religion with older folk religions, such hybridization of ideology tends to occur.

For a good example of this in practice today, all one has to do is look to the island of Haiti, where residents incorporate aspects of the West African indigenous religion of Voodou (a separate but related religion to Voodoo) with Catholicism. In Port-au-Prince, Haiti, it is a common sight to see a Voodou priestess create a Voodou shrine with a statue of the biblical Mother Mary sitting right on top. In much the same way, Malians mixed elements of their ancient ancestral religious practices with Islam.

At any rate, with the festivities in place and the good luck charms at the ready, Mansa Musa's birthday celebration was about to begin. To mark the occasion, the so-called "royal orchestra" came together to perform songs that were meant to capture the experience of making a trip across the desert to reach the holy site of Mecca. This was literally traveling music, which made use of the dynamic pounding of drums to represent their footsteps and rhythmic blowing of horns. The music flowed as freely as the wind at their backs.

Along with the musicians, the wild animals roaming about the outskirts of Gourara no doubt added to the mystique as they howled and called out as the evening progressed. The music, of course, was also accompanied by gleeful dancing, which followed the reverberating sounds in a specifically orchestrated manner. It was in the midst of all of this that the great monarch, Mansa Musa, was given his birthday gifts.

Among the gifts bestowed were the customary sacrificial goat, golden jewelry, precious stones, and a specially made talisman that was uniquely crafted for the occasion. It was similar to the other ceremonial animal horns that were prepared that day, but this horn is said to have been encased in silver and filled with dirt delivered from the capital. It, too, also had specially picked scripture from the Quran, which was chosen for the purpose of blessing the journey.

Mansa Musa was then gifted with a brand-new Quran. He was also gifted with plenty of slaves, which was the custom at the time. But as was previously mentioned, while West Africa has had a long history of slavery, it must be pointed out that the conditions and status of slaves were much different among West Africans than it was when Arabs and Europeans later imposed slavery upon West Africans. For one thing, in many indigenous African societies, it wasn't uncommon for slaves to be elevated to fairly high positions. Yes, they were still owned by someone, but they were also allowed some mobility up the social ladder. This was usually not the case when slavery was carried out in many other parts of the world. Much of the time, even if a slave had been freed, their freedoms were severely restricted and curtailed.

As it pertained to Mali, it would take the Malians quite a long time to shake themselves free from their own legacy of enforced servitude. As late as the 1960s, when modern-day Mali first came into being under Malian President Modibo Keita (an actual descendant of Sundiata Keita himself), Mali was still very much struggling to put a stop to the ancestral practice of Malians having bond servants. President Keita launched massive public campaigns, calling upon anyone still considered to be a slave to be freed. But even with government-backed calls for emancipation, the practice has continued in various forms in Mali to this very day. Apparently, such entrenched traditions are hard to remove outright. And sadly enough, slavery may have been moved underground and thus remains off the periphery, but at least in West Africa, it does indeed still exist.

At any rate, once all of these supposed gifts were bestowed upon Mansa Musa at his birthday celebration, the lore tells us that a lone female singer sang the mansa a song to praise all of the good things that he had done and the good things that he was expected to do in the near future. In some ways, it could be said that this theatrical songstress was actually presenting to everyone the Mali version of a "state of the union address" since it was basically a telling—or presentation—of the current state of the empire set to song.

Just think about it. Much like a president would get up before Congress and laud all of their accomplishments for that particular year, along with what they planned to achieve in the next, Mansa Musa's personal bard likewise sang of Musa's achievements, as well as the goals yet to be fulfilled. It was after all of this that those in attendance were finally allowed to take part in the big feast that had been prepared, and they drank and ate in honor of their beloved ruler.

Chapter 5 – Mansa Musa Makes His Move

"They load their camels at late dawn, and march until the sun has risen, its light has become bright in the air, and the heat on the ground has become severe. Then they put their loads down, hobble their camels, unfasten their baggage and stretch awnings to give some shade from the scorching heat and the hot winds of midday. When the sun begins to decline and sink in the west, they set off. They march for the rest of the day, and keep going until nightfall, when they encamp at whatever place they have reached. Thus the traveling of merchants who enter the county of the Sudan is according to this pattern. They do not deviate from it, because the sun kills with its heat those who run the risk of marching at midday."

-Ibn Battuta

After leaving the festivities of Gourara behind, Mansa Musa and his entourage headed back onto the trail. They still had thousands of miles to go, and in between, they stopped at several regions and towns similar to Gourara along the way. Although the mansa's birthday had passed, they were still greeted by frequent celebrations and gift-giving. They were soon halfway to the first major milestone—the oasis of Touat (also spelled as Tuat). The oasis of Touat is located in a North African region that today lies in the modern-day nation state of Algeria.

In between these two mile markers, Mansa Musa and his traveling party ventured across a landscape that ranged from sand dunes to rough grasslands where wild animals grazed. The emptiness of the countryside was only occasionally interrupted by some ragtag caravan camps or even the occasional stray Bedouin traveler. And as was the case when Mansa Musa and company arrived at the settlement of Teghaza (or Taghaza), they also encountered whole mosques of salt.

This region, in fact, is full of salt mines, and it was not uncommon to find whole houses made out of salt, with perhaps an animal skin roof thrown on top for cover. Once Mansa Musa reached the edge of the oasis of Touat, he and his party celebrated, as the company could finally refill their goatskin bags with fresh water and, for once, could actually rest under the shade of a palm tree or two.

In this region, Mansa Musa also took time to get to know the local leaders. It is said that during these exchanges, Mansa Musa was generous as usual, handing out large amounts of gold coinage to all who sought his audience. In the name of hospitality, he too was given gifts. At one point, he received a precious box filled with pearls. At the oasis, he was given a large supply of a valuable herb called tacarghaut, which is quite renowned for its aroma.

Mansa Musa was also given a tour by the local governor of the wells from which the water of the oasis had sprung. Just before leaving Touat, Mansa Musa took the time to meet with traders who had just arrived from the cities of Fez and Marrakech, located in modern-day Morocco and located just north of where Mansa Musa was at the time. Mansa Musa was interested in both their trade goods and the tales of their travels.

Morocco was an important regional player, and it actually bordered the reaches of Mansa Musa's own kingdom, so he was very much interested in strengthening political and commercial ties with it. Indeed, much of Mansa Musa's life and the lives of several of his successors would be spent prioritizing the diplomatic relations with the Moroccan sultanate above all else. Part of the reasoning behind this focus was due to economic trade. There was also the fear that the Moroccan forces might aggressively swoop down on vulnerable northern frontiers of the Mali Empire as well.

In fact, centuries later, it would be Moroccan military adventurism that would eventually rip important previously Malian-controlled trade cities, such as Timbuktu and Gao, from the Malian orbit for good. Having said that, as shrewd of a ruler as Mansa Musa was, he knew how important securing his northern frontiers were, so he knew that this meant being able to deal with the Mali Empire's northern neighbor, Morocco, on a friendly basis. And in his efforts of dealing with the Moroccans, Mansa Musa was willing to send his emissaries to sultans as well as common, everyday local traders if he felt it would help him keep an ear to the ground to the rumblings of Moroccan ambition.

It was shortly after this consultation with the local traders that Mansa Musa and his entourage once again picked up and began to trek across the desert. Their next stop would be the town of Ghat in Libya. After passing through Ghat, the instances of human habitation would become fewer and farther between.

During this period, it was much easier for doubts and disagreements to surface, and it has been recorded that the mansa's court had to convene to settle arbitrary matters much more frequently during this stage of the journey. Nevertheless, the general impetus to reach Mecca was never in question, and whatever petty disagreements arose, they were eventually settled. In these instances, Mansa Musa played the role of the ultimate arbitrator, and he attempted to be as light-handed as he could when dealing with the problems of his people.

It is said that when Mansa Musa was pushed by some of his advisors to take a firmer hand with some of his more disagreeable subjects, he took it all in stride and instead quoted from scripture, "He who makes the pilgrimage neither cohabits nor errs—nor contests during his pilgrimage. Here, Allah loves peace makers." As one can see, Mansa Musa sought to present himself as a great peacemaker as he traversed across the vast desert sands of North Africa.

In truth, to keep the cohesion of his traveling party, Mansa Musa would need all of the peacemaking and diplomatic skills at his disposal. This was demonstrated later on the journey when a very startling bit of bad luck befell Mansa Musa's caravan. They were out on the open road again when several members of Mansa Musa's party were inflicted by snake bites. Such things can certainly be deadly out in the open desert, and perhaps even worse than the few who might perish is the threat of fear and panic that such an event can spread through the ranks.

It is said that those who were bitten were in horrible condition, screaming and writhing on the ground as the venom coursed through their body. Court physicians tried their best to treat the injured with traditional remedies, such as applying goat milk and cutting open the wounds with knives that had been heated up in the fire. But unfortunately, this age-old method of cleansing snake bites seemed to have very little effect. And as those stricken worsened, with some even perishing, the fears of the whole group increased.

Soon, there were whispers that snakes had infested the whole caravan and were even holed up in the bags of food and other items the group carried with them. If one so much as opened a bag of grain, there would have been a fear that a snake could suddenly spring forth and strike the hand unfortunate enough to have opened it. In such a fearful environment, snakes were everywhere. Sticks became snakes, ropes were pythons, and even a sudden play of shadows across the desert seemed to become venomous vipers ready to strike.

Wild gossip began to circulate that the whole desert might be impassable due to the snakes. And soon, some even openly spoke of turning back. For those familiar with scripture, this series of events almost seems to parallel the biblical story of Moses in the desert with the children of Israel. In this account, Moses's followers were suddenly waylaid by snakes after bitterly complaining that they wished to turn back.

Considering the similarity, it is indeed somewhat ironic that Mansa Musa, whose very name "Musa" is the Arabic form of Moses, faced just such a dilemma. But that is not to say that the event did not occur or was somehow borrowed from scripture. After all, getting bit by a snake in the desert is a common enough occurrence, and it could happen to just about anyone.

At any rate, in such a climate of fear, it took all of Mansa Musa's skills as a leader to keep his entire group from disintegrating into absolute chaos. According to lore, just as discipline was about to break down entirely, Musa received unexpected aid from a man who had tagged along with the caravan from one of their previous stops. The young man claimed to be knowledgeable in the arts of healing and had a plan to save those dying from the snake bites. He instructed the king to slaughter twelve camels, to cut their stomachs open, and to place the feet and hands of those bitten by the snakes into a camel's belly. All of this was done while those in attendance were directed to repeatedly chant certain passages from the Quran. At first glance, such a thing might seem to be simple superstition. And indeed, the solution employed by the shaman incorporated ancestral beliefs and folk remedies, with Islamic flourishes thrown into the mix. However, it has been said that what this man directed to have done to the injured saved their lives.

Despite the strange theatrics involved, the act of putting wounded limbs into the belly of the camel caused the digestive fluid inside the camel's stomach to react to the venom in the wounds of those stricken. The stomach acid inside the camel's digestive system was able to break down the poison, and after a few hours of being given this treatment, most were able to recover.

It certainly must not have been a pretty sight to see several snakebite victims with their hands and feet stuffed into the bellies of dead camels. But if it had the effect of saving their lives, it was most certainly worth it. This ingenious treatment not only saved the lives of those who had been bitten, but it also no doubt prevented a wider panic—and ultimately dissension—from breaking out in the ranks.

It is said that Mansa Musa was incredibly impressed with the young stranger's knowledge, and from that day forward, he was a trusted member of Musa's court. Even during a great journey such as this, if one was able to prove themselves worthy, Mansa Musa was more than willing to make them a part of his inner circle.

One such subject who proved herself worthy of Mansa Musa's esteem was a slave that he had previously procured who originally hailed as far afield as Baghdad. Not much is known about this young woman—even her very name seems to have been forgotten—but it is said that she was Mansa Musa's favorite among all of his female servants. The more cynical might be inclined to think that the reasoning behind this favoritism might be due to simple physical attraction. The woman was indeed described as being beautiful, but Mansa Musa's affection for her was not only skin-deep. Mansa Musa respected her as a trusted advisor and especially appreciated her ability to recite poetry and verses from the Quran. He also enjoyed the fact that she was from the very heart of the Islamic world, and he depended upon her to fill him in on cultural and ideological issues that he did not understand.

But after Mansa Musa's favorite recited a poem at one of the ruler's dinner parties, the esteem with which she was held began to provoke Mansa Musa's other servants to jealousy. As a result, they began to speak badly about the girl from Baghdad. They spoke angrily of the fact that the mansa was spending so much time with a foreigner and even voiced concern that perhaps state secrets might be passed from Mansa Musa to this exotic slave girl, believing she might be a potential spy. Those concerned that the emperor had been compromised didn't have to worry long, however, because the girl was soon afflicted with a terrible fever and died.

Feverish outbreaks of sickness had been periodically running through the camp for a while, and once one of those viral strains reached the girl from Baghdad, her immune system proved incapable of fending it off. The progress of the caravan was momentarily stopped so that the mansa—in his great sadness—could bury his favorite servant. As her funeral rites commenced, the ruler was remembered to have remarked on just how grieved he felt to know that he would never be able to speak to his special friend again.

Since the Malian emperor was generally supposed to be detached from his subjects, this must have been quite an amazing sight for the Malians to see. The emperor typically presented himself in a stoic, if not slightly cold, fashion. The people were not used to their ruler showing outward emotion or even much outward affection at all, and here he was, pouring his heart out over the body of his dead servant.

Mansa Musa had his court dig a grave for the girl right there in the Sahara Desert, and with her body wrapped in the leaves from a palm tree, she was put into the ground and laid to rest. It is said that she was set down on her side so that she was facing Mecca. Even though she wouldn't survive the journey to the holy city, she would eternally rest with her face toward it.

Chapter 6 – In the Land of Egypt

"There is no need for a traveler on the Nile to take any provision with him, because whenever he wishes to descend on the bank he may do so, for ablutions, prayers, purchasing provisions, or any other purpose. There is a continuous series of bazaars from the city of Alexandria to Cairo. Cities and villages succeed one another along its banks without interruption and have no equal in the inhabited world, nor is any river known whose basin is so intensively cultivated as that of the Nile. There is no river on Earth but it which is called a sea."

-Ibn Battuta

After a long journey in the desert, Mansa Musa and his entourage finally reached the land of Egypt, where they set up camp just outside of the famed pyramids. They waited here until an official sent by Al-Nasir Muhammad, the Sultan of Egypt and Syria, came to officially invite the Malian emperor to have an audience with the sultan at his palace. This visit by the sultan's envoy was, of course, followed by the customary round of gift-giving.

In the Arab world, hospitality between a host and their prospective guests is considered sacrosanct. It is said that this notion of a heavy emphasis on meeting the needs of visitors harkens back to ancient times when it was considered one's duty to aid those traveling through the harsh desert terrain. This was done in the hopes that one would similarly be honored when they themselves were in the same predicament.

For a weary traveler who may not have enough food or even water to last them for the duration of their journey, the idea that they could depend on local hospitality to help them through their ordeal was not only a nicety but an actual necessity. This common aid among desert dwellers soon morphed into a complex ritual of hosts meeting the needs of their guests, which can still be seen in Arab households to this very day.

Upon his arrival in Cairo, Egypt, Mansa Musa, as a visiting king, was immediately considered the personal guest of the sultan, and he was endowed with gifts and amenities considered worthy of a man of his station. He was given a grand copy of the Quran with brilliantly illuminated pages, with blue, red, and gold lettering. He was also gifted with a couple of grand chandeliers for his palace back home and a set of special glass bottles with inscriptions from the Quran, among other things.

These gifts were then generously reciprocated by Mansa Musa, as he gave the sultan plenty of gold and other priceless treasures. But Mansa Musa didn't end there. Along with giving gifts to the Egyptian sultan, Mansa Musa decided that he wanted to bestow gifts upon the general populace of Egypt as well. In what seems like some ancient humanitarian mission, the great Malian emperor arranged to have gifts of clothes and food distributed to the poor and homeless masses who lived on Cairo's streets.

The fact that Mansa Musa would engage in such a humanitarian act shows that he not only knew the plight of the poor in Egypt in advance but that he was also willing to do something about it. This was a fact that was surely not forgotten among the thankful recipients, who were given more aid by this visiting stranger than they had ever been given from their own potentate, the sultan.

Such a great act of random kindness would be something like billionaire Bill Gates suddenly popping up on the southside of Chicago and handing out thousands of dollars at a time to all the folks who sleep under bridges and call back alley dumpsters home. This golden bedecked Malian emperor seeking out Egypt's down and out just to hand them fistfuls of gold must have truly been a sight to behold.

As it pertained to the diplomatic front, after a few more back-and-forth dialogues between representatives of Mansa Musa and the sultan, Mansa Musa was invited to come to the palace before the upcoming Friday prayer. Mansa Musa initially tried to get out of making an appearance, stating that he was traveling through the region for purely religious reasons and did not want to have to create any unnecessary commotion by having the sultan play host for him and his entourage. But along with the age-old excuse of a guest not wanting to put a host out, there was another reason that Mansa Musa did not want to visit the sultan. He knew that it was the custom of those paying respect to the sultan to kneel before him on the ground. Mansa Musa, being a great king and not willing to bow to any other man, did not wish to do this out of principle. Yet, as a guest of the sultan, certain court customs were expected to be observed. This was the dilemma that Mansa Musa faced.

However, as Sultan Al-Nasir Muhammad's officials kept pestering Musa to see the sultan, Mansa Musa came up with a plan. He was going to bow to the earth when he was before the sultan, but he was going to do so as he loudly gave thanks to God, thereby showing that he was not bowing to the sultan as much as he was bowing to God. This may seem like a bit of somersaulting semantics here, but for Mansa Musa, the difference was important, and he saw it as the only way he could go and meet with the sultan.

Once this was decided, Mansa Musa then took select members of his entourage with him to go to the sultan's court. This group was met and flanked by the sultan's guardsmen, who escorted them to the king's palace. The denizens of Cairo gathered in the streets to witness the grand procession. They were amazed to see this man from Mali, sitting astride a majestic, white horse, wearing a fine fur cloak with golden embroidery and a silken turban, inlaid with diamonds and gems.

Mansa Musa and his entourage arrived in the courtyard of the palace before being led up to the personal chambers of the sultan himself. Upon seeing Mansa Musa, the sultan, who was seated on his throne, stood up and began to walk toward the emperor of Mali. Mansa Musa then kneeled down on the floor, and as planned, he loudly declared in Arabic, "I prostrate myself before Allah, who created me and brought me into this world," making it clear to everyone within earshot that he was not prostrating himself before the sultan but rather God himself. The sultan then offered the hearty rejoinder, "Allah is great! And Muhammad is his prophet!" After these things were said, the two men greeted each other, and then Sultan Al-Nasir Muhammad led Mansa Musa to sit right beside him as an equal.

Even though they sat right next to each other, the two men usually did not speak directly to one another. Instead, Mansa Musa spoke to the sultan through his translator. This was not so much because Mansa Musa's Arabic was rusty; by all accounts, he was quite fluent. It was simply done out of tradition. Mansa Musa always spoke through his translator when he held court at home, and he continued to do so while he held court abroad. This practice later caused some friction with certain dignitaries who found it insulting, but it was simply a part of Mansa Musa's normal protocol.

At any rate, through this court official, the sultan learned that Mali was indeed a rich realm of abundance. The sultan was informed of the massive gold deposits, salt mines, and the great forests that produced valuable timber. The sultan was also intrigued to know that Islam was rapidly growing in West Africa. Mansa Musa, in the meantime, expressed through his translator his admiration of Cairo's many monuments and mosques. He especially appreciated the ornate stained glass windows, which apparently had just been installed in many of the main mosques recently. To these compliments, Sultan Al-Nasir Muhammad is said to have replied at length:

My brother, your words touch me profoundly. Indeed, our works and those of our predecessors exist only for the glory of our Lord and the well-being of our subjects accordingly to the dictates of the Prophet. I also know the extent of your works, the multiplication of the houses of God on your travels to Timbuktu, to Doukourei, to Goudam, to Dierei, to Quanko to Bako, your generosity toward the peoples you met along your route, your care for the most destitute as instructed by the Prophet. It is our intention to remake our city. These works are made possible by the peace which reigns in the Empire, all the way to the far-off lands of India where our cousin, the Mameluke Sultan of Delhi, reigns. The prosperity of these times follows a long period of penury, of food shortage, and epidemics; our present political stability follows a painful succession of coups and usurpations of which many were extremely violent. I myself was forced to cede power on two occasions. The poem of Ibn Mougha, the father of our literature, born in Baghdad, expresses beautifully what I underwent then: "Fortune frowned on me for a half-day: no more was needed for my friend to flee, putting as much distance as possible between themselves and me." Those days are over. Peace at home and peace abroad are henceforth one. Tolerance is shown to all religious minorities and foreigners who keep their own system of justice for the management of their own internal affairs, but our justice is the same for all. The special laws which applied to them have been abolished. We are at pains to mete out justice personally twice weekly. We hear the plea, question the plaintiffs and rule by seeking to approach the fairness of God. Our Capital speaks every language of the world, some people believe that the genius of man is unlimited and that his achievements are and will be as well. These people are blasphemers! The highways from Byzantium to Mecca, from Tripoli to Tabriz, from Grenada to Jerusalem are all secure.

These words must be taken with a large grain of salt (perhaps one of the largest grains ever to have been extracted from one of Mali's salt mines) since historians know full well just how dangerous travel was in those days. After all, if the roads were really that secure, pilgrims on the hajj would not have had to constantly worry about being ambushed by bandits along the way. Even Mansa Musa, with his vast entourage that included thousands of troops, eventually became susceptible to this very sort of predation. Anyone who strayed away from the main group was likely to be snatched up like stray sheep by wolves on the prowl.

To be clear, this is by no means hyperbole on the part of this writer. Even the Arab scholar Ibn Khaldun readily recorded how, when Mansa Musa eventually began his return trip from Mecca, part of Mansa Musa's caravan got cut off from the main group, and many were kidnapped and even enslaved by Bedouin raiders. But we will discuss this matter in depth a little later in this book.

After their dialogue came to an end, Sultan Al-Nasir Muhammad informed Mansa Musa that he had a whole palace prepared for him near the Mameluke tombs, located in the vicinity of Mount Moggataru. He was also informed that as soon as he and his companions had rested enough, restocked their provisions, and were ready to resume their pilgrimage, he would have his officials help to protect and guide their caravan to Mecca. From his perch at his new palace in Cairo, Mansa Musa temporarily became an additional head of state in Egypt next to the sultan himself.

And as a head of state, Mansa Musa held court and received dignitaries. It was in this capacity that he held an audience with the Abbasid calif of Baghdad. With him, Mansa Musa discussed many aspects of Islamic ideology as well as general philosophies of life. Mansa Musa was also keenly interested in the latest developments in science and mathematics. After all, during this period, Egypt was a great center of learning when it came to both.

The Islamic world had inherited advanced concepts from both Greece and India, and Arab scholars had perfected these concepts even further. The Arabs borrowed the idea of numerals (1,2,3,4) from India, for example, but were able to streamline their use with the creation of new mathematical systems, such as algebra. The name "algebra" itself comes from Arabic.

As anyone who has studied Arabic knows, the word "al" is the Arab equivalent of "the." Al-Jazeera, a popular news program broadcast from the Arab world, for example, means "The Island," which is in reference to Qatar, where the news station first took root. It should be noted that Qatar is technically a peninsula and not an island, though. Another example that's much more infamous would be the terrorist group Al-Qaeda, which translates as "The Base."

Having said that, one might easily conclude that "Al-Gebra" might simply mean "The Math." But as neat and tidy as that might sound, that is not the case. "Al-Gebra," roughly translated, is a phrase that means "The reunion of broken parts." And if you think of what algebra actually does, with all of its formulas and equations that seek to find solutions by plugging in various variables, it is indeed a reunion of broken parts.

Mansa Musa, who was a lifelong scholar, was quite fascinated with all of these aspects of higher learning available to him in Cairo. And considering all of the purchases he was making in Egypt, it was probably a good thing that he learned a little math along the way.

During his stay in Cairo, Mansa Musa engaged in spent much money buying supplies and provisions. Among the more expensive items were extravagant book covers for the Quran, composed of fine materials such as lace and ebony; prayer rugs; and painted glass showcasing brightly illuminated passages from the Quran. Mansa Musa also regularly sent court officials out to the major shopping bazaars in Egypt to get plenty of fine spices, such as myrrh, camphor, and nutmeg, some of it coming as far afield as Indonesia in Southeast Asia.

Some of the other more extravagant items that Mansa Musa purchased were a few magnetic compasses that had been made in China. The compass was still a fairly novel invention, and the idea that a traveler who had one in their possession would always be able to make their way north (at least magnetic north) was a real confidence booster for any journey. With such equipment, at least some fear of ending up completely lost during a sandstorm in the desert could be somewhat alleviated.

Incredibly enough, by the time Mansa Musa was through shelling out gold (all of his purchases were made in raw gold pieces) in Egypt, he managed to crash the whole gold market in the region. This was caused not just by his purchases but also by his generous donations of gold. It is said that Mansa Musa managed to put a dent in the overall value of gold in Egypt by as much as 25 percent.

Part of this massive influx was brought on by greedy Egyptians, as the sellers routinely marked up their wares, hoping that the rich would pay more for much less. And for the most part, Mansa Musa did just that, often paying five times as much for an item than it was actually worth.

Although Mansa Musa tended to turn a blind eye to this price gouging, many of those traveling with him took note, and it has been said that this unfair treatment was remembered long after Mansa

Musa and his court returned to Mali. The memory of this offense, which has been recorded in Malian lore, as well as the actual Egyptian records of Mansa Musa's heavy use of gold, which crashed the Egyptian economy, certainly paints an interesting picture.

Even more interesting perhaps have been the subsequent theories proposed to offer an alternate explanation as to what Mansa Musa might have really been up to. It has long been suggested that it was Mansa Musa's innocent, almost child-like generosity that inadvertently crashed Cairo's economy. Other historians, however, beg to differ. Citing the fact that Mansa Musa was a highly intelligent and even shrewd politician, some have theorized that Mansa Musa knew exactly what he was doing.

According to this line of thought, Mansa Musa might not have been as kindhearted as we believe and that he actually crashed Egypt's economy on purpose! Why would Mansa Musa do such a thing? Well, as it turns out, Egypt was a direct competitor in the gold markets at the time, and by exerting control over it—by way of flooding its markets with excess gold—Mansa Musa was able to take out an economic rival. And while doing so, he appeared to be completely blameless, as he played these acts off as an extraordinarily generous gesture of a great king.

If this was indeed Mansa Musa's intentions, his crafty scheme worked like a charm. Egypt's economy took several years to recover, and Mali's gold markets continued to dominate the world. And in the meantime, Mansa Musa's famous "generosity" cemented him as an international legend. Is this why there appears to be a knowing smirk on Mansa Musa's portrait on the Catalan Atlas? One can only wonder.

Chapter 7 – Mansa Resumes His Pilgrimage

"The people fasted for three successive days, the last of which was a Thursday. At the end of this period, the amirs, sharifs, qadis, doctors of the Law, and all other classes of the people in their several degrees, assembled in the Great mosque, until it was filled to overflowing with them, and spent Thursday night there in prayers and liturgies and supplications. Then, after performing the dawn prayer–they all went out together on foot carrying Qurans in their hands–the amirs too, barefooted. The entire population of the city joined in the exodus, male and female, small and large, the Jews went out with their book and the law and the Christians with their Gospel, their women and children with them; the whole concourse of them in tears and humble supplications, imploring the favor of God through his books and his prophets."

-Ibn Battuta

Mansa Musa and his court left Cairo as the Egyptian summer turned to fall, staying for about three months in total. Mansa Musa left with just about as much fanfare as with which he had arrived, and the Egyptian people would not soon forget him. Mansa Musa and his companions soon crossed the Red Sea and entered Saudi

Arabia itself. The sultan of Egypt had called ahead of his guest and made sure that special depots with additional provisions would be set up along the way.

The sultan had also made sure that military leaders in the region were aware that the pilgrimage was taking place and put out instructions that the pilgrims be carefully looked after. Compared to the struggle of crossing the Sahara Desert in North Africa, this well-provisioned and well-attended last leg of the journey was much easier. Before reaching Mecca, Mansa Musa and company made a stop in Medina, the town in which the Prophet Muhammad's mortal remains rest.

Here, Mansa Musa visited the fabled Green Mosque, where both the prophet and a couple of the original caliphs—Abu Bakr and Umar—were entombed. It was shortly after Mansa Musa paid his respects in Medina that the caravan was able to make it to the outskirts of the Saudi Arabian city of Mecca—the main focal point of all of Islam. As Mansa Musa's entourage approached, it was, once again, quite a spectacle for the locals to behold.

Mansa Musa's mobile palace was a grand tent encampment, as Mansa Musa's kingly tent was flanked by thousands of other tents for his followers. There were also countless pack animals carrying all manner of provisions, as well as gifts both received and those yet to be given. Mansa Musa's own generosity when it came to gift-giving was quite well known by then.

Upon entering the city of Mecca, each one of these visitors had to buy a special pass or "visa" in order to enter the city. These passes worked much like a modern-day visa, allowing travelers to have temporary official permission to remain in the region. Once this was acquired, the pilgrims could pass freely into the great city of Mecca. During this procession, some rode on the backs of camels, but many more walked on their own two feet.

Mecca was an impressive sight to see in those days, but even before the rise of Islam, the city of Mecca was a major hub in the region. Mecca served as a trading outpost for various neighboring regions, such as Yemen, Ethiopia, Syria, the Byzantine Empire, and even far-away India.

As Mansa Musa and his fellow pilgrims made their way through Mecca, they made sure to follow all of the traditional rules and rituals that were expected of pilgrims as they approached the Great Mosque of Mecca, which houses the religious shrine of the Kaaba. The hajj itself is supposed to demonstrate the solidarity of Muslims in their reverence of God as they march in lockstep to the Kaaba, which is considered to represent "Bayt Allah," or as it would be in English, the "House of God."

It is not so much that Muslims literally believe that God calls the forty-three-foot-high, thirty-six-foot-wide cube-shaped structure home as much as it represents the presence of God to the Muslim faithful. And as Mansa Musa made his way to the structure, he was no doubt in the company of countless devout Muslims from all over the Islamic world.

Once inside the Great Mosque, Mansa Musa and those with him would have walked around the Kaaba seven times in a counter-clockwise direction. Although the ritual is mainly done in commemoration of Muhammad's supposed final journey from the site of the Kaaba to the Al-Aqsa Mosque in Jerusalem and then on to heaven, it is believed that the tradition dates back to Abraham.

Abraham is said to have visited the valley of Mecca, where his son, Ishmael, had been taken in prior years by the handmaiden whom Abraham had impregnated—Hagar. According to Islamic lore, the archangel Gabriel, who helped guide Ishmael and his mother Hagar through the desert, gave the child a black rock, which then ended up inside the Kaaba. A black stone still resides in the Kaaba to this day, which visitors touch to receive a blessing. Some believe that the rock is actually part of a meteorite.

In pre-Islamic times, when the locals were primarily polytheists who worshiped a wide variety of deities, the structure of the Kaaba was actually a shelter in which various stone idols were stored for a multiplicity of local religious practices. In that sense, it is somewhat ironic that Muhammad would eventually consecrate the shrine for Islam, as the religion is steadfastly against idolatry.

At any rate, as it pertains to Mansa Musa, his pilgrimage was filled with many moments of surprise and discovery. During his hajj, he made more of the big purchases he had become famous for, buying a couple hundred prayer rugs, as well as 150 religious manuscripts, all paid with, once again, a vast amount of gold. In all, Mansa Musa's pilgrimage in Mecca lasted for twelve days. During this time, he made sure to wear the all-white, spotless garments of a pilgrim. He also made sure to take off his flashy gold and jewels and put them to the side before he neared the Kaaba since a pilgrim on the hajj—even a powerful king such as Mansa Musa—is expected to be modest.

It was in this garb that Mansa Musa entered the great mosque, touched the black stone, drank from precious fountains, bowed to the ground in prayer, and circled the Kaaba in the procession of faithful believers. After taking part in the procession around the Kaaba, Mansa Musa ended up staying in the city of Mecca for a few more months. So, while the pilgrimage itself lasted for twelve days, Mansa Musa stayed on as a visitor to the city a few months after that.

During this time, Mansa Musa embarked upon a campaign to get the Meccan authorities to allow him to bring a few "descendants" of Muhammad back with him. In Islam, especially in ancient times, men who could claim descendance from Muhammad were revered as devout teachers of Islam. And Mansa Musa wanted to bring a few of them back to his realm so that they could help better instill

Islamic tradition in the Mali Empire. Initially, the grand sharif, who was in charge of such matters, refused to allow any such thing. It took some time and a bit of a pressure campaign on the part of Mansa Musa's diplomatic representatives, but finally, the Meccan authorities relented and decreed that if one of the descendants wished to travel with Mansa Musa, they would be permitted to do so.

Once this permission was granted, Mansa Musa made sure to create as much incentive as possible. He had it announced that he would hand out a small fortune in gold to any descendant of Muhammad who would make the journey with him back to Mali. Due to his generosity, he ended up having four descendants of Muhammad agree to join his caravan. He also met a lot of other interesting people, including a famed architect from Spanish Granada named Abu-Ishaq Ibrahim-es-Saheli. This architect would actually be convinced to travel back to Mali with Mansa Musa's entourage, and upon his arrival to the Mali Empire, he was commissioned to build several grand mosques and other structures and monuments. The Spanish Muslim would use techniques that blended both classic European and Arab design, as well as unique and astonishing innovations that were all his own.

Upon his return home, Mansa Musa was proud that he was now an official hajji, and he was determined to bring back as much of the wonder he had experienced to his own homeland. But before he sent his caravan back toward Mali, he had a special private meeting with his most trusted griot to record some very important thoughts that had intruded upon his mind.

As the griot sat and listened to what his sovereign had to say, Mansa Musa reported, "I should carry myself before you like the happiest man in the world. We have crossed half the world without a major trial, apart from the death of my favorite slave [the woman from Baghdad] and the loss of a score of our companions. We have been received everywhere according to our station, welcomed, supported, and protected. We have seen, in the latter regard, how other sovereigns act, their traditions and their works. As you so love to say: In due time, we will do as the bees, making the same honey from many different flowers. We have acquired objects of great import for the material and spiritual well-being of our subjects. During our absence, our kingdom has known peace and prosperity."

After Mansa Musa continued at some length about all of the accomplishments that had been achieved, the old griot gave his own forecast of what the future might hold. The griot declared, "Our sons and the sons of our sons and their sons will know terrible times. They will be forced outside of the equality of all men. But no matter where they are, they will retain in their hearts and in their minds the hope born of your long voyage, and of all you have evoked, such as your reception according to your rank. Where ever they may be, they will keep in their hearts and in their minds the hope born of your pilgrimage."

Some have interpreted these sayings to be a kind of prophecy of things to come. It could be seen as an interpretation of a time in the future in which Mali would be subjugated and brought under the yoke of foreign oppression. And this would indeed happen to Mali in the centuries to come, as enemies from abroad would take advantage of an increasingly splintered Malian civilization.

In that sense, it seems that the old griot was prophesying to Mansa Musa that even in those dark days ahead, Malians will always look back at the days of greatness under his reign and be proud. As the griot contends, wherever Malians may be, no matter where their diaspora may take them, they will always look back on the epic pilgrimage that Mansa Musa made, and their hearts and minds will be filled with hope for their future and immense pride for their past.

Chapter 8 – Heading Back Home

"We kissed the holy stone; we performed a prayer of two bowings at the Maqam Ibrahim and clung to the curtains of the Kaaba at the Multazam between the door and the black stone, where prayer is answered; we drank of the water of Zamzam. Then having run between al-Safa and al-Marwa, we took up our lodging there in a house near the Gate of Ibrahim."

-Ibn Battuta

Mansa Musa may have been the richest man in the world, but by the time he got back to Cairo, Egypt, he was flat broke. It had been a rough trip between Mecca and Cairo, and at one point, Mansa Musa and his core group of followers became separated from the rest. They ended up being so lost that even Mansa Musa's Chinese compasses failed to regain their bearings.

Caught in a sandstorm in the middle of the desert, one becomes quite easily disoriented. Mansa Musa and his fellow lost companions ended up making their way out to the Suez (the later site of the Suez Canal). Here, they were able to survive on whatever they could fish out of the waters, but the situation was downright grim. There were bandits lurking everywhere, waiting to strike weary, worn-out, and lost travelers just like Mansa Musa and his entourage. Anyone who lingered too far from the pack was indeed ambushed and forced into slavery.

Just imagine being out fishing for some food for your dinner only to have a Bedouin charge at you, tie you up, and throw you on the back of a camel. It certainly wasn't much fun for those who were captured, that's for sure. Fortunately for many of these hapless victims of the Bedouin, the name and fame of Mansa Musa were enough to gain the release of many. But even for those who were not kidnapped, the threat of dying out on the desert would claim many.

Mansa Musa needed more cash in order to continue provisioning his caravan for the journey home to Mali, so he resorted to taking out loans from Egyptian financiers. One of those financiers was a man by the name of Siraj al-Din. Although his pockets were currently empty, Siraj knew that Mansa Musa had more than enough money waiting for him back home. Even so, in order to ensure that Mansa Musa would make good on paying back the money he had lent, he arranged to have one of his own representatives (or some would say bill collectors) join Mansa Musa's entourage for the trip back to Mali. However, as it turned out, Siraj al-Din's loan officer got cold feet and backed out at the last minute. This left Siraj al-Din with the choice of either fully putting his trust into the Malian emperor to keep his word and repay him or to go along for the ride himself. Siraj al-Din was a crafty businessman, and he wasn't about to leave his repayment to fate, so he ended up joining the caravan and traveling back to Mali with the monarch himself.

He also made the decision to have his son join him on the journey. It would later prove wise that he did so since Siraj al-Din died during the trip. Some would later speculate that the money broker was poisoned. But the motive for such an act remains unclear. Mansa Musa himself certainly would not have had the man killed, as this would have been completely out of character for him. It also would not make much sense since Mansa Musa had more than enough money back home to repay the broker.

At any rate, since Siraj al-Din's son had come along for the journey, he was more than able to collect on his father's behalf. It was also Siraj al-Din's son who helped to squelch rumors that his father had been assassinated. Siraj al-Din's son insisted that his father's death was a natural one, reminding those who jumped to conclusions that he had dined on the same portions of supposed poisoned fare that his father had, yet he was none the worse for wear. In the end, this son would be able to finish the journey to Mali, and he would be given what his father had been owed in full, proving that Mansa Musa had no reason to cause any harm.

The death of Siraj al-Din caused much unwarranted drama, but Mansa Musa was also in for some good news too. On his way back home, he received the astonishing tidings that his great general, Sagamandia, had not only put down an insurgency in the region of Gao but that he had also managed to completely annex Gao to the Mali Empire.

Mansa Musa was delighted at the news, and he would later begin several building projects in the region, including the great Gao Mosque, which can still be visited this very day. This mosque serves as a lasting testament to the greatness of his rule, as do other structures that were erected by Mansa Musa. Mansa Musa had a reach that extended far and wide, and his fame reached the ears of all who resided within the boundaries of his sprawling dominion.

Gao, which had long been a rich and prosperous region due to its abundance of copper and salt, was a real boon to Mansa Musa. Gao was actually founded by fishermen in the 7th century, and it went on to become one of the greatest centers of trade in West Africa. Gao then became the capital city of the thriving Songhai

Empire in the early 1000s. Under Songhai dominion, the city of Gao was a thriving outpost, trading copper, gold, salt, and even slaves.

The region was strategically and geographically important, as it controlled a major portion of the Niger River. It was also a kind of breadbasket since the land was fertile, and there was also a rich capacity for agriculture. Mansa Musa, who was elated to hear of these developments, decided to make an immediate detour on his journey back to the Malian capital and made his way directly to Gao instead. He planned to meet with the recently deposed king of Gao and affirm his leadership over the region. He also had intentions of taking the king's two princely sons as "hostages."

As hostile or even downright criminal as such an act might sound today, the taking of royal hostages was actually a common practice in those days. A royal hostage was taken from a deposed potentate in order to ensure the deposed leader's future cooperation. It was kind of an insurance policy that would prevent the defeated party from doing anything rash while the conquering authorities were away. Royal hostages were always well taken care of, but they were still technically prisoners in gilded cages, used for the purpose of ensuring stability in recently annexed territories.

On his way to Gao, Mansa Musa made a pitstop at the city of Ghadames. This settlement was located in modern-day Libya, and it boasted a Roman fortress dating back several centuries. Here, it is said that Mansa Musa met an interesting character, a desert commander who was engaged in guerilla raids against enemy tribes in the region of Wargala (also spelled as Ouargla). This renegade apparently sought an audience with the Malian emperor to see if he would be interested in assisting his war efforts against Wargala. The official lore grows silent as to what—if anything—came of such war plans. The guerilla commander, however, is remembered as having left Ghadames to journey on with Mansa Musa to the region of Gao.

At any rate, when Mansa Musa arrived at the gates of Gao, he was greeted by the king, who agreed to hand over his two princely sons—Suleiman Nar and Ali Kolon—as royal hostages. Even with the loss of Gao, the Songhai Empire carried on, and it would wait in the wings for its chance to reclaim lost ground.

As important as Gao may have been, it was the capture of Timbuktu that would prove the most pivotal. At the time, Timbuktu was only second in importance for the Songhai Empire, with Gao as the most important, but Mansa Musa would come to make Timbuktu eclipse and ultimately surpass Gao in many ways. Mansa Musa renovated the city and allowed it to become a major trading hub and weigh station between several North African trade routes, connecting places such as Fez, Morocco, and Cairo, Egypt, to towns such as Tuat and Ghadames.

But as important to trade as Timbuktu would become, Mansa Musa also made it a focal point for education. He installed several mosques, universities, and other cultural centers in the city. Mansa Musa turned Timbuktu into a vast repository for all of the wonderful things that he had learned during his hajj. It was Mansa Musa, after all, who installed the Sankore center of learning, which would later lead to the University of Sankore.

These institutions would not only serve as learning centers for those who lived in the region but also for any Islamic scholars willing to make the trek and learn abroad. And as the renown of the institutions grew, many would indeed become willing to make that journey. Mansa Musa put Abu-Ishaq Ibrahim-es-Saheli—the Grenadian architect who had chosen to come to the Mali Empire with Musa—to work over the next few years, building all kinds of mosques, memorials, and institutions of learning in Timbuktu and Gao.

Many of these are now considered World Heritage Sites, and in 1990, the city of Timbuktu itself ended up on the World Heritage List of Endangered Places, courtesy of UNESCO (United Nations Educational, Scientific and Cultural Organization). Unfortunately, several were vandalized, and some were completely destroyed in the 2010s by radical Islamic extremists. Three of the so-called "sacred tombs," which belonged to past Malian leaders—Sidi Mahmoud, Sidi Moctar, and Alpha Moya—were some of the sites completely destroyed by the looters.

The most important work that Abu-Ishaq Ibrahim-es-Saheli constructed in Timbuktu was the Djinguereber Mosque, which was completed in 1327. The structure is quite unique because it has a framework of wooden timber that protrudes out of the walls. The desert terrain of Timbuktu often makes for a dynamic and even unusual setting, and these unique structures, with wooden planks sticking out of them like some kind of desert porcupines, further adds to the otherworldly experience.

Another great building project that was commissioned during this period was a palace called the Madugu, which would be Mansa Musa's home away from home when visiting the city. It is said that Abu-Ishaq Ibrahim-es-Saheli received a handsome amount of gold for his efforts.

Once Mansa Musa set these great things in motion, he finally began to prepare for the journey back to the capital of the Mali Empire—Niani. Mansa Musa opted to put many of the women, as well as some of the Islamic scholars who had traveled with him, on boats to sail down the local Niger River, while Mansa Musa and the main contingent would continue back to the capital overland. This decision would cause some unexpected drama when Dian, which was a vassal state of Mali at the time, attacked the ships as they sailed past. The lord of Dian was apparently planning on taking everyone prisoner, but once he realized just how distinguished his hostages were, he decided to let them go on their way. Mansa Musa and his entourage all safely returned to the capital city with more than their fair share of stories to tell.

Chapter 9 – Return to the Capital

"The people of Mali outnumbered the peoples of the Sudan in their neighborhood and dominated the whole region. Their authority became mighty and all the peoples of the Sudan stood in awe of them."

-Ibn Khaldun

Upon his return to the capital city of Niani, Mansa Musa, fresh off the hajj, was galvanized to strengthen the Islamic influence in his realm. Despite the fact that Mansa Musa was a Muslim and that Islam had more or less become the official state religion, there were still great pockets of resistance to the Muslim faith. Many in his realm still held firm to their ancestral beliefs, and some even openly practiced the dark arts of wizardry and witchcraft.

Such things, of course, are in complete contradiction to Islam. The Quran memorably condemns magic and magicians in its account of Moses facing off against the Egyptian pharaoh's sorcerers. In the Quran, Moses is called "Musa," so it is somewhat ironic that Mansa Musa's namesake is used in one of the Quran's most powerful denunciations of magic. The Quran recounts the biblical story as originally told in Exodus when Moses stood before the pharaoh and his court magicians cast down their rods only for them to transform into snakes. Moses then cast down his staff, and it became an even bigger snake, ostensibly not through magic but through the power of God, allowing Moses (or Musa) to defeat the pharaoh's magicians.

Or as Surah 20:65-70 reports:

They said: Oh Musa! Will you cast, or shall we be the first who cast down? He said: Nay! Cast down. Then lo! Their cords and their rods—it was imaged to him on account of their magic as if they were running. So Musa conceived in his mind a fear. We said: Fear not, surely you shall be the uppermost. And cast down what is in your right hand; it shall devour what they have wrought. They have wrought only the plan of a magician, and the magician shall not be successful wheresoever he may come from. And the magicians were cast down making obeisance; they said: We believe in the Lord of Haroun [Aaron] and Musa [Moses].

As such, Mansa Musa, who had become a dedicated Muslim by this point, was deeply troubled by his own people's resistance in becoming dedicated to the Islamic faith. It seems that many of the hybridized Islamic and pagan practices, which didn't bother Musa before, were troubling to him upon his return. Now, even something as simple as burying one's loved ones created a problem because Mansa Musa had learned the proper last rites that were to be conducted for Muslims, and this tradition was most certainly at odds with what most citizens of the Mali Empire did.

In Mali, the usual custom as it pertained to the burial of the deceased was to have a small funeral service and then simply leave the dead exposed in the bushy wilderness so that nature could take its course. Mansa Musa's Islamic scholars were not too pleased to learn of such things, to say the least. Mansa Musa leaned heavily on the learned men of Islam who had returned home with him, trusting them to instill the religion and culture of what it meant to be a Muslim in his people. He had them institute Islamic prayers on Friday, Islamic dietary laws, social customs, and the like.

Along with making sure that the people were educated about Islam by his Islamic scholars, Mansa Musa also wished to further cement his power by having his favorite architect, Abu-Ishaq Ibrahim-es-Saheli, construct a grand palace for him in Niani. This building would stand out from the rest due to its heavy use of plaster, which was a unique building material in the region at that time. The building was vast, with a special audience hall, courtyard, and other fixtures. The windows stood out for their frames, which were lined in both silver and gold. Abu-Ishaq Ibrahim-es-Saheli was once again handsomely rewarded with his efforts by being given plenty of gold and other gifts and personal perks for the skills that he demonstrated.

Despite all of Mansa Musa's great works, life for the average person in his kingdom remained relatively the same. The average person still continued to live on a diet of mostly rice and a few various fruits and vegetables, and they drank water straight from the local rivers, just as their ancestors before them had done. In the searing Malian heat, most lived in the cool confines of mud dwellings. The mud structures were lined with animal fat, which was also often turned into soap and even used to make torchlights. The biggest, most lasting impact that Mansa Musa had on the lives of the average Malian, however, was the enshrinement of Islam in their hearts. After Mansa Musa returned from his pilgrimage, his efforts of Islamization paid off, and soon, people of all walks of life were attending Friday evening prayer services at their local mosque.

Efforts were also made to study the Quran. Not only that, many attempted to commit the entire Quran to memory, and they instilled this virtue in their children as well. As brutal as it might sound, some parents even put their kids in chains until they had satisfactorily memorized their verses! Arab Scholar Ibn Battuta supposedly witnessed this practice firsthand. He would later recall, "They place fetters on their children if there appears on their part a failure to memorize the Quran, and they are not undone until they memorize it." Call it hands-on parenting or call it horrible abuse, but one thing is for certain—Malian parents were apparently very eager to have their offspring knowledgeable about the Quran. But although Islam became more dominant in the region, some would always hold onto aspects of their ancestral religions. It was also hard for Malians to conform to the more patriarchal structure of Islam.

In Mali, for example, it was common for men and women who were not married to talk with each other freely as equals. Such things, however, were considered anathema to certain tenants of Islam and were not to be permitted. What also most certainly wouldn't have been permitted, at least according to conservative Muslims, was the naked dancing that took place in many traditional festival activities in Mali. Some Muslim visitors, such as Ibn Battuta, took offense to the extravagant demonstrations of ancestral rituals mixed with Islamic practice.

Ibn reported his disgust at seeing "royal poets who romped about in feathers and bird masks," for example, expressing his wish that stricter Islamic protocol be followed in the Mali Empire. Some of Mansa Musa's Islamic scholars who were imported from abroad were indeed quite shocked and horrified to see such practices in place. Mansa Musa, who was undoubtedly embarrassed and concerned that he might lose prestige among his Muslim peers, more than likely cracked down on such excesses as he strengthened the hold of Islam in his kingdom.

Along with making sure that his subjects were educated in Islam, Mansa Musa also wanted to make sure that his own son was equipped to follow in his footsteps after he was gone. Mansa Musa had actually hoped that his son might take over for him even before he died so that he could essentially retire to Saudi Arabia, where he planned to spend his life as a humble monk, renouncing all things of this world. But before he could embark upon any kind of early retirement, Mansa Musa knew that he still had some unfinished business to settle.

By this point, Mansa Musa was quite famous, with whispers of the rich king reaching ears in Italy and Portugal. Soon, these two countries were both competing with Islamic powerbrokers to have access to trade with Mali. Mali's conduct with Portugal actually kicked off the Portuguese desire to explore the west coast of the African continent. But perhaps the most important political alliance that Mansa Musa struck was when he reached out to Abu al-Hasan, who ruled the central Maghreb.

Mansa Musa sent an envoy to the powerful ruler to open up trade relations, and Abu al-Hasan heartily agreed. He knew of Mansa Musa's great reputation and his kingdom's enormous wealth in gold, so he was more than willing to open up a dialogue on trade. He sent the envoys back with both his blessing and several expensive gifts. Mansa Musa, however, would not get to receive them, as he passed away in 1337 before his envoy returned home.

Mansa Musa, like all of us, didn't know the day or the hour of his passing, and he most certainly figured that he had several more years left than he actually did. After all, he was not sick, and by all accounts, his demise was an abrupt and sudden one. And although his son, Mansa Maghan, had filled in for his father in the past and ostensibly had been groomed to succeed him, at this juncture, he seemed a bit unprepared. Being a mansa of such a sprawling empire, after all, is indeed a heavy load to bear. And for whatever reason, Mansa Maghan just no longer seemed up for the challenge. He actually ended up only ruling a few short years before his uncle, Mansa Musa's brother, Mansa Sulayman (also spelled as Suleyman), stepped in to take over.

Chapter 10 – Mali after Mansa Musa

"Whenever a hero adds to the list of his exploits from conquest, Mansa Musa gives them a pair of wide trousers. The greater the number of a Dogari's exploits, the bigger the size of this trousers."

-Al-Dukhari

The Mali Empire was rocked by the news of the great monarch Mansa Musa's abrupt passing in 1337. But as shocking as the loss of this great leader may have been, the Mali Empire initially seemed to be in a good position for a seamless transfer of power since Mansa Musa's son, Maghan, had already been groomed to replace him. But although he had served as an able steward when he filled in for Mansa Musa during his pilgrimage to Mecca, Mansa Maghan proved to be an inept ruler over the long haul.

Unfortunately, or perhaps fortunately considering his ineptitude, after facing a wide variety of problems during his rule, he ended up perishing just a few years later. This occurred around 1341, and that same year, he was replaced on the throne by his own uncle, Sulayman. Sulayman was Mansa Musa's brother, and many hoped that he would prove to be as capable as his sibling when it came to his ability to run the empire.

Mansa Sulayman did show some of the same qualities as his brother in his ability to govern, but he never gained the affection of the public as Mansa Musa did. On the contrary, according to historian David C. Conrad, Mansa Sulayman was not just unpopular but "intensely disliked." There is some indication that Mansa Sulayman was viewed as a usurper even though his placement on the throne would appear to be more a matter of fate than one of political intrigue. It seems the severe dislike that Mansa Sulayman generated among the Malian masses emerged early on, although it is still not entirely clear why Mansa Sulayman struck such a chord with the public. It seems that no matter what this mansa did, his people would always view him as an evil usurper and illegitimate leader.

Nevertheless, whether the people liked him or not, Mansa Sulayman sought to continue right where his brother, Mansa Musa, had left off. It was indeed Sulayman who would establish official relations with Abu al-Hasan of Morocco, just as his late brother Musa had so desired. And Mansa Sulayman, no doubt wishing to show a similar sense of generosity as his deceased brother, held an extravagant welcome party for the first official representatives of Morocco who came to visit.

Unlike Mansa Musa, Mansa Sulayman didn't hesitate to make himself subservient to the sultan, and the Moroccan diplomats went back to Morocco, telling their potentate that Mansa Sulayman was ready to "pay duties" to the sultan and demonstrate his submission. Mansa Sulayman was apparently willing to bow his head if he thought it would gain him a powerful ally.

Mansa Musa, as can be seen in the chapter above when he refused to kneel before the sultan of Cairo (he kneeled to God instead), was not willing to make himself anything other than an equal to his peers on the international stage. Mansa Sulayman had inherited much uncertainty when he came to the throne, however, and he probably figured he could use all the help he could get.

His powerful ally would not remain on the scene for long, though, as a revolution rocked Morocco shortly thereafter. In this popular uprising, Abu al-Hasan was dethroned, captured, and whipped. Many of his troops were killed, and his navy was destroyed. Abu al-Hasan was forced to step down, and his son took over what was left of his father's kingdom. Abu al-Hasan perished in 1351. He was largely disgraced at this point, but his one loyal friend, Mansa Sulayman, held a grand remembrance ceremony in his honor.

Arab scholar Ibn Battuta, who was in Mali for the occasion, vividly recalled the event. He was amazed at both the extravagance and the way in which Islamic and African ancestral traditions merged together. Some elements were similar to what he had observed at countless other Muslim memorials for deceased kings, but other aspects were completely unique to the nature of Mali at this point in history.

As a firsthand eyewitness, Ibn Battuta tells us the following:

[The sultan] has a lofty pavilion, of which the door is inside his house, where he sits from most of the time. There came forth from the gate of the palace about 300 slaves, some carrying in their hands bows and others having in their hands short lances and shields. Then two saddled and bridled horses are brought, with two rams which, they say, are effective against the evil eye. Dugha the interpreter stands at the gate of the council-place wearing fine garments of silk brocade and other materials, and on his head a turban with fringes which they have a novel way of winding. The troops governors, young men, slaves, the Masufa, and others sit outside the council place in a broad street where there are trees. Inside the council place beneath the arches a man is standing. Anyone who wishes to address the sultan addresses Dugha and Dugha addresses that man standing and that man standing addresses the sultan. If one of them addresses the sultan and the latter replies he uncovers the clothes from his back and sprinkles dust on his head and back, like one washing himself with water. I used to marvel how their eyes did not become blinded.

After the death of Abu al-Hasan, Mansa Sulayman was never able to recapture his previous good relations with Morocco. And from there on out, any real ties between the two increasingly became none existent. Rather than having a powerful friend, Mansa Sulayman would come to fear a resurgent and powerful Morocco to the north. As Mansa Musa himself had often feared, the growing threat of Morocco would become an increasing problem for the Mali Empire in the future.

Mansa Sulayman's kingdom, in the meantime, was already becoming fragmented, if not geographically, at least politically. Not everyone agreed with Sulayman replacing Mansa Musa's son Maghan, and as such, from the very beginning of his reign, not everyone supported the new emperor. When the famed Arab scholar Ibn Battuta paid a visit, he too must have soaked up much of the Malian public's disdain for the current mansa. It seems that when he first reached out to the mansa's court, he, too, became disenchanted with the monarch.

It appears that the start of Ibn Battuta's disenchantment with Mansa Sulayman occurred shortly after he contacted the emperor's royal representatives. Under normal protocol, a visiting dignitary such as Ibn Battuta would have been accorded a special welcome, which would include generous presents. Ibn Battuta no doubt knew all about the previous Mali emperor's great generosity, and he likely expected to receive something similar in kind. He was shocked when, instead of being given gifts of gold, he was just given a few loaves of bread, some beef, and a gourd filled with a hearty helping of yogurt.

He was at home when one of his fellow scholars informed him that representatives from the mansa's court had delivered a few gifts. As Ibn Battuta described it, "I got up, thinking that it would be robes of honor and money, but behold! It was three loaves of bread and a piece of beef fried in gharti [shea butter] and a gourd containing yoghurt. When I saw it, I laughed, and was long astonished at their [the Malians] feeble intellect and their respect for mean things."

It sounds pretty comical, but Ibn Battuta was downright insulted. So much so, in fact, that he dared to complain to Mansa Sulayman himself. Just imagine Ibn Battuta complaining to the great Malian leader, shouting, "Are you kidding me? I came here all the way across the Sahara, and all you have for me is a pound of beef and a couple of loaves of moldy bread?" Of course, that dialogue was a bit of an artistic flourish on this writer's part, but one can only imagine how palpable the indignation of this Arab scholar must have been.

In reality, he did not lodge his grievance directly and instead relayed his message through an envoy, and Ibn Battuta's complaint was a little more diplomatic (although still entirely indignant) than it might have been depicted above. Ibn Battuta, who followed the advice of the mansa's own griot, a court figure called "Dugha," whom Ibn referenced in his previous observations of the memorial service for the dead Moroccan sultan, gave the emperor a piece of his mind. In an official complaint sent to Mansa Sulayman, Ibn charged, "I have journeyed to the countries of the world and met their kings. I have been four months in your country without your giving me a reception gift or anything else. What shall I say of you in the presence of other sultans?"

It must have been somewhat shocking for Ibn Battuta to lodge such a complaint in regard to the mansa's hospitality. It is also a little troubling that Ibn Battuta seems to belittle him as a mere sultan when Malian mansas sought to be recognized as something more than that—they wanted to be known as powerful emperors.

Mansa Musa, after all, considered himself to be at a higher level even than the sultan of Cairo. There was a reason why Musa famously refused to bow and kiss the sultan's hand, as other more subservient kings would have done. Having said that, in some ways, Ibn Battuta's words seem to have at least some measure of blatant disrespect.

Such a disrespectful discourse to an all-powerful emperor might seem pretty bold, but Ibn Battuta, who fearlessly traveled the world, was a bold person. And at least, in this case, his temerity paid off, as it has been said that by the time that he finally decided to depart company with the mansa in February of 1353, he was able to leave with his saddlebags full of "one hundred mithqals of gold."

It's important to note that the monetary unit known as the "mithqal" was actually a derivative of the Syrian currency known as the "dinar," which originated in the form of golden coins. It is said that when similar gold coins came into use in West Africa, they became known as "mithqals." Some say that the mithqal typically weighed around 4.25 grams. But this was not always the case, and there was always some variation in what a mithqal may have actually represented. Regardless, Ibn Battuta walked away with a good amount of gold.

Despite Sulayman's later gesture of goodwill, Ibn Battuta never forgot the slight and later wrote about Sulayman, saying that he was "a miserly king from whom no great donation is to be expected." But to be fair, Mansa Sulayman may have just been trying to be practical. Times were a bit different in his day than they were during the reign of Mansa Musa. Mansa Sulayman had inherited an empire much larger than the one that Mansa Musa had to contend with when he first came to the throne. Mansa Sulayman's "miserliness" was perhaps due to his concern of maintaining the cost to govern the huge frontiers of his empire.

According to West African scholar and historian William B. Noseworthy, this was a constant dilemma that Mansa Musa's successors faced. As Noseworthy puts it, "The later mansas of his [Mansa Musa] lineage struggled variously with control over the imperial economy: if they tightened spending, they would appear miserly; if they overspent, they would not retain enough funds to expand the empire." It was a sort of darned if you do and darned if you don't mentality that a lot of mansas faced when it came to the handling of their finances.

Mansa Sulayman was obviously worried about spending, and his perceived miserliness was most likely merely a kind of pragmatic caution on his part. In many ways, after all, it is much easier to build an empire than to maintain it. From the Romans to the Byzantines, from Genghis Khan to Tamerlane, all of the great sprawling empires of the world seem to be at their greatest when its rulers are still growing and annexing new territory. It is holding onto the annexed territory that becomes the hard part.

Despite his unpopularity, during his reign, Mansa Sulayman seemed well positioned for this task of consolidation. It is said that his reign was generally a peaceful and prosperous one. He still had much wealth as it pertained to gold, copper, and salt mines. From the northern Malian city of Teghaza alone, Mansa Sulayman regularly pulled in tremendous profits from the salt that was being mined. Ibn Battuta, who visited the town during his stay in the Mali Empire, famously complained, "This is a village with nothing good about it. It is the most fly-ridden of places!"

But fly traps like these brought in steady revenue for the kingdom all the same. So, it most certainly wasn't that Mansa Sulayman was broke when it came to his reasoning behind his perceived stinginess; it seems he was just trying to conserve as many resources as he could. And, as was demonstrated by Ibn Battuta's colorful testimony, with a little effort, Mansa Sulayman could still be goaded into acts of huge generosity all the same.

Before he left, Ibn Battuta also got his fair share of scandal and intrigue from the royal court. During his famous visit to the mansa's court, Ibn Battuta witnessed a falling out between Mansa Sulayman and his wife, Qasa (also spelled as Kassi). Although the mansa of the Mali Empire commonly had more than one wife, Qasa was considered to be the main royal bride of Mansa Sulayman. She was actually the niece of one of Sulayman's uncles, which made her of the royal line.

Somehow, she had fallen out of the king's favor, and Mansa Sulayman actually had her arrested and thrown in what constituted as the jailhouse. She was soon released, however, and relegated to a kind of house (or in this case palace) arrest, during which time she was closely monitored and even forced to cover her face with a veil. In the meantime, the mansa had taken a new wife by the name of Banju, who had no royal relations. Mansa Sulayman was apparently infatuated with his young new wife Banju, despite the fact that the Malian court was against it.

In fact, the mansa's advisors even went so far as to have a quiet talk with Mansa Sulayman, hoping that he would reconsider Qasa's punishment, but Mansa Sulayman refused, insisting that she had been found guilty of a grave offense. Mansa Sulayman claimed that a personal servant of Qasa was interrogated about suspicions of Qasa plotting against the king. The servant, who was bound hand and foot and subjected to questioning, allegedly confessed that Qasa was actively plotting with the king's cousin to see if he might help her depose Mansa Sulayman, pledging that the army would aid them in the cause.

It is said that once Mansa Sulayman explained these happenings to his court, they heartily agreed that the queen got what she deserved. Not only that, they insisted that if it was true, she must be put to the sword immediately. Mansa Sulayman was not willing to go that far and instead insisted on banishing her from royal affairs. Qasa would go on to live in a local mosque, where she apparently lived out the rest of her life in quiet penance and reflection.

Rather than seeming like a tyrant, Mansa Sulayman actually seemed merciful. But the question remains: was Qasa really plotting against her husband? Did her servant really testify to this? And if so, was it a false confession brought on by the duress of the interrogation? Sadly, as with most other aspects of African history, it seems that we will probably never really know for sure.

But whatever the case may be, Sulayman's carefully orchestrated reactions during the ensuing fallout and chaos enabled him to calm his rattled court officials, prevent a possible rebellion, and save a whole lot of face in the process. From here on out, Mansa Sulayman managed to regain some of the stability that his sibling Mansa Musa had enjoyed, and he would continue to rule as the emperor for another twenty-four years.

After his death, which occurred sometime around 1360, the Mali Empire was engaged in a war of succession. This arose over disputes to the throne, with Sulayman's heir, Kanba (who also happens to sometimes be called Qasa or Kassa), and Mansa Maghan's son, Mari Diata II (also spelled as Mari Djata), each claiming the right to sit upon it. Although the details are a bit murky, it seems that Mansa Kanba may have been the relative with whom Queen Qasa had been plotting to overthrow Mansa Sulayman. At any rate, Mansa Kanba was killed after ruling Mali for less than nine months. After Mansa Kanba died, Mari Diata II ultimately came to power.

Mari Diata II would have some staying power during his time as mansa, as he remained on the throne for fourteen years. But during this time, he was widely remembered as a tyrannical leader who terribly oppressed his own subjects. He was also known as a rather frivolous, if not downright incompetent, despot who wasted precious resources.

On one occasion, for example, he supposedly sold a giant rock of pure gold, which was of immense worth, to a group of Egyptian merchants for a small fraction of its price. This feat of such squander most certainly would have had the penny-pinching Mansa Sulayman rolling over in his grave.

According to an Arab scholar named Ibn Khaldun (not to be confused with Ibn Battuta), who spoke with some of the king's subjects on the matter, most were completely aghast at what Mari Diata II was doing. Ibn Khaldun interviewed one man who is reported to have related that Mari Diata II "ruined their empire, squandered their treasure, and all but demolished the edifice of their rule."

Mansa Musa, of course, was known for his goodwill in giving away gold or even buying some provisions at marked-up rates, but Mari Diata II's hawking of this solid gold rock was apparently just considered completely pointless. Mansa Mari Diata II's rule would come to an end when he perished in his sleep in 1374. His son, who happened to be named Musa, came to power next.

But by the time of Mansa Musa II, the Mali Empire was nothing like it had been under Mansa Musa I. According to Mali historian David Conrad, Mansa Musa II was actually known to be a "just, wise, and considerate ruler," which was in stark contrast to his tyrannical predecessor, Mari Diata II. But unfortunately, Musa II just didn't seem to have the strength (or stomach) to hold the Mali Empire together.

Sometime in the middle of his reign, he opted to delegate most of his duties to a court official named Mari Jata (not to be confused with Mari Diata II). Under these conditions, Mansa Musa II was still the head of state, but his actual power was very limited. Nevertheless, his fill-in, Mari Jata, did his best to stabilize the kingdom. Among other things, he stationed troops in the Sahara Desert to keep important copper and salt mines around the city of

Takedda from slipping out of the Mali Empire's grasp. For a time, he also restored authority over the eastern reaches of the empire that had since begun to break away. However, it was often an uphill struggle just to keep order in these far-flung frontiers.

In the midst of this backdrop of uncertainty, Mansa Musa II died in 1387. Mansa Musa II's brother, Mansa Maghan II, would then attempt to maintain order after Mansa Musa II's demise. He would prove even more uncomfortable with leadership, and for the short year that he reigned, he largely left major decisions up to his court ministers.

Mansa Maghan apparently died sometime in 1388, although no one seems quite sure what may have happened to him. Considering the tumultuous state of affairs in the royal capital, he very well could have been assassinated, perhaps poisoned by some court schemer. He may have also died from the so-called "sleeping sickness" that was known to befall people of all walks of life at any time during those days.

What Malians called "sleeping sickness" was actually a lethal illness that was spread by tsetse flies. These pests, which are about the size of a horsefly, actually gain their nourishment from blood, and they frequently make a snack out of grazing cattle, as well as human beings. Through this blood sucking, a dangerous parasite that lives in the fly's stomach can be transmitted, which can lead to an illness called trypanosomiasis. The illness progressively affects the victim's nervous system, and it is not uncommon for one who is affected to suddenly stop breathing in their sleep. It is for this reason that those who perish from the disease are said to have died from "sleeping sickness." Having said that, it could very well be possible that Mansa Maghan simply died in his sleep, the victim of nothing more than an errant fly that had buzzed unseen into his quarters. It has been said that countless people in the region today still fall prey to this ever-present hazard.

At any rate, after Mansa Maghan's passing, he was replaced by an ambitious court official named Sandaki. Although he was not of royal blood, he actually attempted to put some legitimacy on his reign by marrying Mansa Musa II's mother. It doesn't seem that these efforts did him much good, however, as he was assassinated a short time later. After the death of Sandaki, the empire was once again in chaos, with several factions fighting for the throne.

Amidst this turmoil, a man named Mahmud clawed his way to power in the year 1390. Unlike the usurping Sandaki, Mansa Mahmud (also known as Mansa Maghan III) had some royal blood in his veins. In fact, he could claim direct heredity from the first great Mali ruler—Sundiata Kieta. Having said that, not a whole lot is known about Mansa Mahmud's rule.

It seems that around this point, Mali became a much more isolated place, and as a result, outside commentary on the empire would become almost nonexistent. Mansa Mahmud would be the very last emperor of Mali to be specifically mentioned by name by Arab historians. After this last known mansa, who sprung from the Sundiata family tree, all available resources on Mali's subsequent imperial line seem to go completely dark. The truth is, during this period, there is a whole lot that we just don't know.

The situation only seems to deteriorate at this point, and it is recorded that the great city of Timbuktu slipped from Mali's grip in 1433. Although not many records of what happened exist, it seems that the city of Gao had already broken away a short time prior to Timbuktu leaving Mali's orbit. If Mansa Musa had lived to see all of this, he most certainly would have been heartbroken, especially considering all of the efforts he had spent in constructing majestic mosques and dynamic centers of learning in these frontiers of the former Mali Empire.

The next major phase of the Mali Empire's collapse occurred in 1460 when one of the so-called "kings" of Gao—a man who went by the name of Sulayman Dama—launched an assault on the city of Mema. After the fall of Timbuktu and Gao, Mema had become the Mali Empire's easternmost province and a storied one at that. For it was here, in the city of Mema, after all, that the great Mansa Sundiata Kiata and his noble mother, Sogolon Conde, had fled to seek refuge during a time of dynastic turmoil.

Needless to say, it came as a shock when Mema was ripped out of the Malian orbit. Mema was one of the first major provinces to become joined to the early Mali Empire, and now even Mema was lost. The Gao leader Sulayman Dama, who successfully wrested all of these lands from Mali, then proceeded to pass all of his territorial gains on to his successor, Sii Ali Beeri.

Sii Ali Beeri would carve out his own empire from the carcass of Mali and develop the next major power player in West Africa—a completely resurgent Songhai Empire. Sii Ali Beeri is said to have been an ingenious military commander, and his many successes in battle were partly due to his use of a fearsome cavalry that utilized well-armed soldiers on horseback who could quickly smash into enemy flanks. These horses were bred with the famed Barbary breed, which Bedouin raiders used on their lightning raids. Along with the rapid deployment of his horses, Sii Ali Beeri also made use of the local waterways to transport his infantry on riverboats upstream and downstream for quick mobilization.

Although Sii Ali Beeri may be considered a villain to modern-day Malians, for the Songhai, he is still considered to be a heroic figure. He is reverently known as "za beri wandu," which translates as "the great and dangerous Za." Although he was ostensibly a Muslim, Songhai storytellers contend that he was also a powerful sorcerer, hence all that talk about him being "the great and dangerous Za."

At any rate, Sii Ali Beeri was quite successful when it came to the consolidation of the gains of Gao and Timbuktu, and he forcefully reinstituted Songhai control over many of the regions' gold and salt mines. Sii Ali Beeri would go on to rule his reconstituted realm until he perished in 1492. Yes, the very year that Christopher Columbus was sailing across the Atlantic on a mission that would end up with the European discovery of the Americas, the former Mali Empire was being cast to the side by their old rival, the Songhai.

The resuscitated Songhai Empire would prove to be short-lived, however, since they were later wiped off the map by Morocco in 1591, which had invaded from the north. The fabled city of Timbuktu—Mansa Musa's pride and joy—then came under the administration of Morocco. Thus, previous Malian emperors such as Mansa Musa and Mansa Sulayman proved to be quite correct in their fear of attack from Morocco. The attack the Moroccan army launched against the Songhai in the spring of 1591 was said to have been particularly devastating. At this point, the Moroccans were well armed with muskets imported from Spain, as well as an early handgun called an arquebus. They also had some cannons that were capable of lobbing stone cannonballs.

For their part, the Songhai, who still relied largely upon the classic bow and arrow, spears, and swords, were simply no match for the upgraded weaponry of the Moroccan armed forces. The ruler of the Songhai during this time, Askia Ishaq, apparently saw the writing on the wall and attempted to literally buy himself some time. He sent a dispatch to the sultan of Morocco and pledged to pay him 100,000 pieces of gold and gift him 1,000 slaves if he would call off the assault. All this did was serve to reinforce just how demoralized and utterly defeated the Songhai were in the sultan's mind. Refusing to recall his troops, the sultan seized upon the military weakness of the Songhai and ordered his troops to seize the Songhai kingdom for Morocco.

As it pertains to the Malian dominion, the small little remnant that ultimately succeeded the Mali Empire would eventually be colonized, not by Moroccans but by Europeans. The French made inroads into what remained of Mali in 1892 during the European barnstorming epoch across the African continent known as the "Scramble for Africa." Prior to this, Mali had managed to limp on as a weak but independent state. Part of the reason behind Mali's continued resistance to colonization was its remote location, which was hard for explorers to reach.

By the late 19th century, however, the French, who already had holdings in the region, readily incorporated Mali with the rest of their colonial territories and christened the entire region as French Sudan. The French colony would then become simply known as French West Africa once more territories were cobbled together.

It is no coincidence that so many people in West Africa speak French today, as the language was imposed in many regions during France's colonization. It is somewhat ironic that much of French West Africa contained the former regions of the Mali Empire, forcing all of the puzzle pieces together that Mansa Musa and so many others had tried so hard to make fit under their own dominion. Mali would remain in this forced union of fellow colonized states until the modern-day independent nation of Mali was born in 1961.

Conclusion: The Legacy of an Empire

Throughout the history of the world, many empires have risen, and many have fallen. It is hard to say what the legacy of an empire should be. But as it pertains to the rulers of these imperial juggernauts, one man seems to stand out among them all—Mansa Musa, the tenth mansa of the Mali Empire. Even though many of the details about his life are rather scant when compared to other great leaders, what we do know is incredibly intriguing.

Mansa Musa came to power after his predecessor, Abu Bakr II, sailed across the Atlantic Ocean, never to be seen or heard from again. Like all things to do with the Mali Empire, the story of how Mansa came to the throne is epic in itself. No one knows what happened to Abu Bakr II, whether he succeeded in reaching "the other side" of the Atlantic or not, but it was on the heels of his incredible voyage that Mansa Musa came to prominence.

All evidence indicates that Mansa Musa was an ambitious king from the very beginning of his reign. He had a great interest in increasing Mali's military might and international trade, as well as in pushing the borders of the Mali Empire to farther frontiers. He also wished to be a wise and just domestic administrator, one who solved disputes and maintained a relative state of peace and order in his kingdom.

Another aspect of Mansa Musa's initiative was his earnest desire to strengthen Mali's ties to the greater Islamic world. As much as his incredible journey across thousands of miles of desert to make a pilgrimage to Mecca was meant to fulfill his personal desire to complete the hajj, he also desired to use his trip to the heart of Islam as a means to forge a lasting bond with traditional Islam.

Mansa Musa's mind was always in consideration of the betterment of his kingdom. But what is often missed about Mansa Musa's life is just how lonely his perch from the pinnacle of the Mali Empire must have been. In the Malian court tradition of the day, the emperor was considered to be so far above everyone else that it made the notion of having close, personal friendships extraordinarily difficult.

As custom dictated, the emperor was not even supposed to talk directly to his associates. All speech was to be transmitted through his court translator. While such dialogue might be almost humorous on some occasions (just imagine how difficult it would be for a mansa to request someone at a royal banquet to pass the salt), when it came to regular routine conversation with an associate, it must have been incredibly cumbersome.

But such measures were not put in place merely to make life more difficult; rather, they were in place out of sheer pragmatism. Part of the reason behind this artificial barrier between the emperor and his subjects, you see, was to make sure that no one near the ruler would unduly influence him or retain any kind of special favor. If every person who spoke to the mansa had to do so through a cumbersome, mechanical process such as this, it created the appearance of formality—nothing more and nothing less but a formal audience with the emperor.

Such formality served to keep the court gossips from assuming that anyone was being treated better than anyone else. That is not to say that these formalities ever broke down. For instance, Mansa Musa highly favored the so-called "woman from Baghdad," and it was clear to all that she was indeed someone who was very special to the emperor. Nevertheless, for the most part, Mansa Musa's daily interactions were usually highly scripted and orchestrated to keep the many tongues of his court ministers from wagging.

Following such a scripted routine must have been an incredibly daunting task, but Mansa Musa fulfilled his role. And he fulfilled it well. He was an incredibly rich and powerful man who held many secrets, and most of these alternate blessings and burdens he shouldered alone. Much of Mansa Musa's greatness lies in the fact that he was able to effectively compartmentalize his own life.

His successors were not quite so easily skilled in this department, and they were often swayed by court intrigue and led astray. His own son and then a whole litany of Mali rulers were toppled by simple excess and homegrown intrigue. And despite all of its immeasurable wealth, in the end, all the money in the world was not enough to keep the Mali Empire from falling apart. Nevertheless, the legacy of Mansa Musa and his empire continues to be imprinted and ingrained upon the Mali people to this very day.

Shortly after Mali gained independence from the French in 1961, they elected their first president: Modibo Keita. Keita was said to have been a direct descendant of that first great Keita who founded the Mali Empire, the powerful mansa Sundiata Keita. Soon after taking office, President Keita commemorated Mali's former greatness by issuing postage stamps that featured the great Sankore Mosque, one of the greatest remaining testaments to the legacy of both Mansa Musa and the Mali Empire itself.

Out of all the conglomerations of states in West Africa, the legacy of Mali is the greatest. It was only the European colony of

French West Africa that came close to matching the territorial scope of the Mali Empire. And for obvious reasons, this forced entity can hardly be considered a cohesive polity by any means. What Mansa Musa and his forefathers, such as Sundiata Keita, accomplished was an incredibly unique feat in world history, and the legacy of the Mali Empire won't soon be forgotten.

Part 2: Timbuktu

A Captivating Guide to an Important Ancient City and How It Became a Part of the Wealthy Mali Empire during the Reign of Mansa Musa

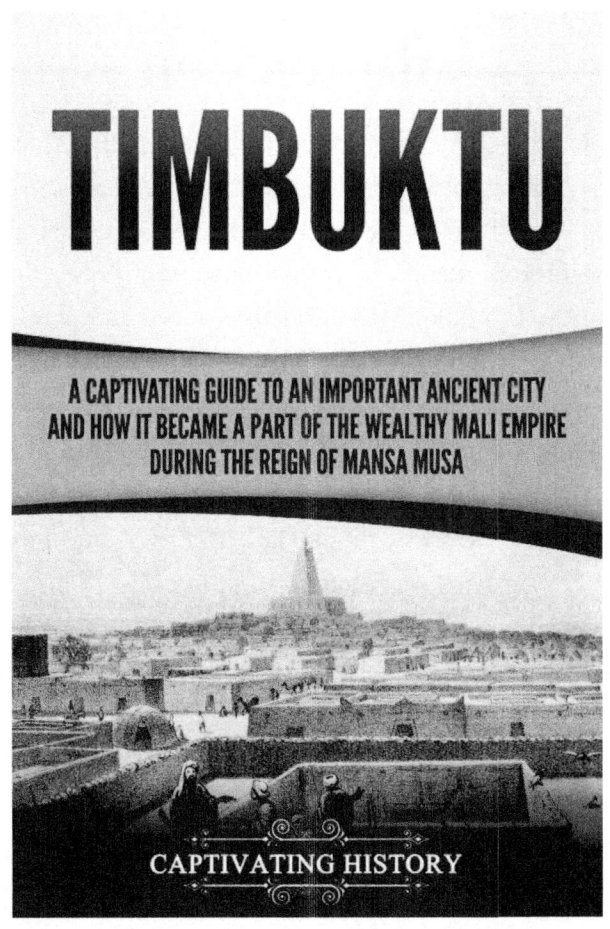

Introduction

Most people in the Western world have heard of Timbuktu, yet it maintains a similar place in their minds as Atlantis, the fictional "sunken city." While claims could be made that Timbuktu has "sunken" (although turned to ruins might be a better description,) unlike Atlantis, Timbuktu was and still is very much a real city, with real inhabitants and an interesting history.

While historians have a pretty good idea of Timbuktu's history, all the details of it are heavily debated, including the actual foundation of the city and the origin of its name. Whether it was founded in the 5th, the 11th, or the 12th century is another matter of contention. Regardless of when it was founded, Timbuktu, once spelled as Timbuctoo, is a city located in modern-day Mali, which is located in West Africa. Founded by the Tuareg people, Timbuktu would develop into an ancient metropolitan. It was home to state-of-the-art schools, libraries, and mosques, and it served as a hub for trade, study, and the arts, sort of like an ancient New York City.

Although most people might not know much about Timbuktu, we are quite familiar with many of its stories and characters. For example, some believe that Mansa Sundiata was one of the primary inspirations for Disney's *The Lion King*, which was also inspired by

William Shakespeare's *Hamlet*. Timbuktu was also the home to perhaps the richest man in history, Mansa Musa, who many may know as the answer to a commonly asked trivia question or one of the inspirations for Marvel's *Black Panther* movies. You may also have heard of Timbuktu for its more recent violent struggles with Islamic terrorist groups or the Tuareg rebellions. If none of these apply to you, perhaps you are familiar with Timbuktu referring to the opposite end of the world. So, how did a city that once housed some of the world's top scholars and artists turn into a synonym for the "middle of nowhere?"

Chapter 1 – Timbuktu's Creation and Its First People (Beginning–13th Century)

Earliest History

As with most cities around the world, very little is known about the earliest years of Timbuktu, and what is known has mostly been discovered recently through archaeology, environmental data, genetics, and language studies. Of course, historians have and will continue to speculate on the mentions of Timbuktu in religious texts, orally passed down stories, and fictional books. Yet, all of these speculations are simply hypotheses on what the ancient history of Timbuktu could have been, and even the more scientific discoveries are constantly being disproved, readjusted, and corrected.

However, despite the lack of concrete evidence on Timbuktu's earliest history, by piecing together various sources of information, historians have attempted to explain how the once nonexistent city just south of the Sahara Desert in what is now Mali grew to become a mecca of trade, riches, and culture by the 16th century. Of course, as with most speculated theories, there is quite a lot of debate surrounding Timbuktu's history, specifically its foundation date and the meaning of its name.

A map of where Timbuktu is located
https://commons.wikimedia.org/wiki/File:Ml-map_(de).png

Some historians believe Timbuktu was founded as early as the 5th century, although the more common thought is that Timbuktu was founded in either the 11th or 12th century. The city is said to have been founded by a nomadic Tuareg woman named something close to Timbuktu's current name, although historians debate whether that name was Bouctou, Timbuctoo, Timbuktu, or Buctoo, along with some other spelling variations.

The meaning of Timbuktu seems to change quite dramatically depending on the version of the founder's name, and there is, once again, a number of theories on the actual original meaning of Timbuktu's name. The main theories are that Timbuktu, whatever its original spelling may be, translates to "place covered by small dunes," "mother with a large navel," "the well of Bouctou," or "the wall of Butu." The final theory is that the name refers to its hidden nature. This variation in meanings has to do with the lack of concrete history of the Tuareg people and their origins, who inhabited the territory in Timbuktu's earliest years.

The Tuaregs

As with the history of Timbuktu and of most people, much is shrouded in mystery, and this is especially true when it comes to the Tuaregs and their indigenous nation-state. It is believed that the first mention of the Tuaregs was by the Greek historian Herodotus (c. 484-c. 425 BCE), who mentioned a people group operating trade routes throughout the Sahara, living in what is known today as southwest Libya. Although he rereferred to this group inhabiting the Fezzan region as the Garamantes, historians today believe he was referring to the Tuaregs. Yet, despite the potential acknowledgment of the Tuaregs' existence as early as the 5th century BCE, very little is actually known about this group, even though they managed to survive for many centuries in one of the world's most severe climates. In fact, the lack of information on their history is often credited to their isolation in the harsh Sahara Desert.

Similar to the history of Timbuktu, most information about the Tuaregs comes from environmental, genetic, and language data. The former indicates that the Tuaregs' habitat of the Sahara, which was once a favorable place to live, transformed from stable living conditions into an extremely harsh climate around five thousand years ago. This shift in the environment likely caused the Tuareg people who had been inhabiting the region to spread out throughout the Sahara to Mali, Niger, Nigeria, and other West

African countries, allowing them to have contact with other groups. This migration and intermingling are confirmed by genetic studies.

The Tuaregs are said to be descendants of an ancient Saharan ethnic group known as the Berbers. The Berbers, whose name originates from the Romans who used the same name for most indigenous Africans they encountered, are native to northwestern Africa and are said to be descendants of another North African, pre-Arab population. Although once again these mentions are speculated, the Berbers' presence was recognized by Europeans as early as 3000 BCE. However, it is very likely that the Berbers existed for centuries before that, as evidence of rock art that resembles that of the Berbers is dated to the oldest possible dates for the region, which some historians believe to be over 100,000 years ago. In Egyptian history, the Egyptians were said to have fought descendants of the Berbers—the Meshwesh and Lebu people—who took over Egypt around 945 BCE. In other words, there was an indigenous North African population that was named the Berbers by the Romans; however, that name is not exactly specific, as all native African populations encountered by the Romans who shared similar political, social, and economic systems at that time were given the same name.

Sometime later, likely many centuries, if not many millennia, after the Saharan Ice Age, a group of the Berbers, who eventually became known as the Tuaregs, developed their own individual culture. They began to spread out throughout the Sahara. On top of the shift in climate, the Tuaregs' migration is also linked to the increase in the exploration of colonists and other invaders, which prompted the indigenous people to emigrate to find resources and trade opportunities. Although the Berbers might have once been sedentary, their original migration caused the group to adopt an almost entirely nomadic culture.

In the 1st century, when camels were first introduced to the Sahara by trade with Saudi Arabia, the Tuareg migration rapidly advanced, as they could move around more efficiently. From North Africa, the Tuaregs spread in all directions, eventually making the over 3,700-mile trek to northwestern Africa to the region where Timbuktu is located. The introduction of camels to the Sahara did more than just speed up the migrations; it also caused the Tuaregs to develop a distinct culture surrounding camel-herding.

Similar to the debate surrounding the meaning and origin of the name Timbuktu, the origin and meaning of the name Tuareg are unclear. The name Tuareg does not originate from the Berber language or people, from which the Tuaregs descended. That being said, some historians believe that Tuareg is derived from the Ḥassānīya Arabic word Twārəg (Tārgi), meaning inhabitant of Targa. Targa was the name used by the Tuareg people for the Fezzan region, which likely derived from a Berber word meaning "drainage channel." Other historians believe that the Tuareg name was given to the people by the Arabs. The two people groups were enemies after the Arabs tried and failed on multiple occasions to convert the native African peoples. Tuareg translates to "abandoned by God" in Arabic.

Despite all the debate surrounding the origin and meaning of the Tuareg name, the group has multiple names for themselves. These include "Imohag," which actually translates to "free men" or "free people"; "Kel Tamajaq," which translates to "speakers of the Tamajaq language"; and "Imajaghan," which translates simply to "Tuareg people." There is no surprise that there are so many names both adopted by and given to the Tuareg, as the ethnic group is spread throughout thousands of miles in northwestern Africa.

And although they often share a similar lineage, communication with other groups, and migration patterns, Tuareg ideologies can differ quite a bit. An example of the similarities and differences in Tuareg populations is in their native language. Tuaregs all speak the same language, but different Tuareg groups have a different name for it. For instance, Tuaregs in the west, specifically in Mali, call it Tamasheq. Tuaregs in Algeria and Libya know it as Tamahaq, and Tuareg populations in the Niger, Azawagh, and Aïr regions refer to the language as Tamajaq. These examples display the differences that can develop as an ethnic group migrates, separates, and develops their own culture within their new location. Regardless of its name, the Tamajaq writing system, known as Tifinagh or Shifinagh, is said to have ancient Libyan, likely Berber roots, confirming the ancestry and migration of the Tuareg people.

The Tuaregs and Timbuktu

Regardless of the debate, historians agree that the city was founded sometime between the year 0 and the year 1100 by a Tuareg person, most likely a woman who served as the group's matriarch, leader, heroine, guardian, or some other important figure. Since the Tuaregs did not have a matriarchal system, nor do they have one today, it is more commonly accepted by historians that Timbuktu's founder was more of a supervisor of the land. They believe she took care of the camp while the actual leader led the explorations. Perhaps she stayed behind because of her skills, or perhaps she was too old to join the expeditions. In some less commonly accepted versions of the history, the city's founding woman was not actually a part of a large tribe but rather ran a camel rest stop in the area. This, of course, would be of necessity to all Tuaregs, as they spent much of their time trekking the harsh climates of the Sahara. Regardless of her actual position in the tribe, Timbuktu's founding woman is still known by the Tuaregs as the "Mother of us all."

Seeing as the Tuaregs were traveling and migrating quite rapidly during the first millennium, there is no surprise that the population eventually reached the territory of Timbuktu and chose to settle there. After all, the location is well placed near the Sahara Desert trade routes and the Niger River. Though Timbuktu would be built up to become a city, it is likely that the nomadic Tuaregs used the territory as more of a seasonal camp for many years, returning to the location as needed. In the meantime, the group continued to roam the desert and surrounding territories during the favorable travel months.

While the Tuaregs were temporarily settled in Timbuktu, they would take advantage of its fertile soils, which were hard to find so close to the Sahara. Because there were few groups actually traveling and surviving in the severe Sahara Desert, the Tuaregs were able to not only claim and keep Timbuktu but also carry items from trading hubs in Egypt and Saudi Arabia to other parts of Africa. Since northern, western, and southern Africa could easily access Timbuktu without having to traverse thousands of miles of the Sahara Desert, Timbuktu quickly became a trading post. It was able to connect Morocco to western Africa for the first time, and it was all controlled by the Tuaregs, who were making the almost impossible trek across the Sahara to bring sought-after goods, such as gold, ivory, and salt to Timbuktu.

During these early years, the Timbuktu trading post was used for more than just exchanging physical products. With so many people gathering in one location, there is no doubt that Timbuktu served as a hub for spreading ideologies, most notably that of Islam. Although the earliest proof of this can be linked to around the 13th century, it is likely that this spreading of religious ideologies was occurring in Timbuktu for many years before. By the 1200s, Muslim texts were certainly being exchanged in the trading city, as were other written and spoken teachings of Islam, such as medicine, law, mathematics, and more. Before long, Timbuktu became a hub of Islamic teachings, and universities of sorts were created to further educate the people of ideologies that were being formed across the Sahara Desert in Cairo, Baghdad, and places even farther away.

Since the largest ethnic population in Timbuktu was the Tuaregs, it is no surprise that the Tuaregs themselves are today predominantly Muslim, though their exact year of conversion is somewhat unclear. After all, the nomadic group had likely encountered many Islamic people by the time Timbuktu became a trading post. Regardless of exactly when the Tuaregs became Muslim, it is certain that by the 16th century, a majority of the Tuareg population identified as Muslim, though their ideologies, even today, differ from other Muslims due to their unique lifestyle and location. For example, the Tuaregs' nomadic travel does not allow for fasts such as that of Ramadan. And while the group may loosely follow the rules, they are more likely to observe feasts. Another key difference in how the Tuaregs observe their religion is that, unlike in most Muslim communities, the men wear veils, not the women. This difference is likely due to the fact that the men did most of the traveling through the Sahara, which required some kind of face covering to protect them from the blowing sand.

Proof of Timbuktu's connection to Islamic teachings is evident in Sankoré Madrasah, also known as the University of Sankoré, which was built in 989 CE. Sankoré was one of the region's earliest madrasahs, which refers to any institution intended for either secular or religious education, no matter the level. Unlike typical universities or religious educational institutions in Europe, Sankoré, like most madrasahs, is made up of many separate schools, which share the same name but are run by a different headmaster.

Since Sankoré was a religious institution, most teachings surrounded the 'Koran, though students could also study other subjects, such as astronomy, logic, and history. Students at Sankoré typically had a single teacher who would teach either in a mosque, an outdoor courtyard, or in their own private residence, allowing students to truly familiarize themselves with their educator's lessons without distractions. Similar to university teachers today, educators and scholars of Sankoré Madrasah wrote their own books, which would actually make up a large portion of Timbuktu's economy. In the earlier days of Timbuktu's trade, only gold and salt made more profit than these educational books. Over the course of Timbuktu's history, Sankoré would house some of the city's and the continent's most incredible thinkers, including Ahmed Baba, who attended the school sometime in the 16th century.

Chapter 2 – The Mali Empire (Around 1200–1255)

Meanwhile, while the Tuaregs were gradually developing Timbuktu into a massive trading hub, the Mali Empire was just forming not too far away. As with the Tuareg people, very little is known about the years preceding the formation of the Mali Empire. What is known for certain is that before the creation of the Mali Empire, there were many small Malinké kingdoms surrounding the upper area of the Niger River, mostly in Ghana. The Malinké is a West African people group divided into many distinctive groups, which formed different kingdoms led by hereditary nobility. The most well-known of these families would be the Kangaba dynasty, which began its rule around the 7th or 8th century. The dynasty was so influential in the early years of the Mali Empire that, at one point, the capital of the empire was in the still-existent town of Kangaba. In the years preceding the creation of the Mali Empire, the various Malinké groups operated independently from one another, even those located near each other.

Sundiata

Sometime in the early 13th century, in the town of Niani located in the Malinké Kingdom of Kangaba, Sundiata Keita, the future creator of the Mali Empire, was born. During Sundiata's early years, much of West Africa was ruled by King Sumanguru, who is depicted as a cruel leader by the many orally transferred epic poems of the time. Sumanguru was originally the leader of the Kingdom of Kaniaga, which was then inhabited by the Susu people. Like most leaders of the time, Sumanguru was hungry for more land and power, and he spent most of his rule attempting to conquer states throughout the Ghana Empire. Rather than focus on his own kingdom, which was in need of attention and stability, Sumanguru continued his ruthless tirade, not caring how many were killed along the way. He finally captured the capital of the Ghana Empire, Kumbi, in 1203.

According to West African oral tradition, Sundiata was one of a dozen noble brothers in line to rule the Kingdom of Kangaba. However, when Sundiata was still a boy, King Sumanguru, who was not yet the ruler of the kingdom, was on his vicious spree of conquering small states throughout West Africa. Sundiata's small town of Niani, located around the modern-day Mali-Guinea border, was also taken over by Sumanguru's military. According to orally passed down epic stories, the Kingdom of Kangaba became overrun by Sumanguru's aggressive men, and they killed the entire royal family, except for Sundiata. At the time, he was quite ill and appeared to be not too far away from death. Eventually, Sundiata recovered from his sickness, and with all of his brothers and most, if not all, of Kangana's leaders dead, Sundiata took on the leadership position of dugu-tigi in a small Kangaba village. Of course, since all of this history comes from orally transmitted epics, much of Sundiata's past may be fictional, as stories can easily be altered through generations of word of mouth.

Despite the debate surrounding Sundiata's origin, what happened after is of little contention. While acting as the leader of this village, Sundiata gained favor amongst his people and began organizing a private army in order to take on Sumanguru's oppressive rule. Unlike Sumanguru, before Sundiata attempted to take on any other kingdoms, he worked to build the approval of his own people, which strengthened his army.

In 1235, Sundiata was finally ready to fight. His army marched toward Sumanguru's, and the groups met in Koulikoro Region, in today's western Mali. The armed confrontation between Sundiata's Malinké people and Sumanguru's Susu people, which came to be known as the Battle of Kirina (Krina), was extremely violent. Sundiata's private army defeated Sumanguru's forces, and while it is unknown as to what became of Sumanguru and whether or not he survived, it is known that Sundiata took the throne. Sundiata quickly consolidated and unified a number of the small Malinké kingdoms, forming what would come to be known as the Mali Empire.

As mentioned above, there is quite a bit of variation in the stories told about Sundiata, and many aspects of his life are often debated. That being said, all variations of the story follow a similar vein. Sundiata was in line for the throne, yet it was snatched up by the cruel Sumanguru. During Sumanguru's reign, Sundiata was cast aside, but he built up his own private army in order to successfully take down Sumanguru and earn his rightful place on the throne. It may sound a bit like a fairytale, a play, or a plot to a movie, and that's because Sundiata's story resembles Disney's *The Lion King*.

In fact, the plot of the kid's movie follows some versions of Sundiata's story even more closely. In one variation of Sundiata's history, his father, King Naré Maghann Konaté, had a rather sickly son who, through preservation and determination, overcame his disabilities and not only learned to walk but also became stronger than other boys his age. When King Naré Maghann Konaté died (if following the Disney plot, he would be Mufasa), there were many members of the family fighting for the throne (although, unlike the Disney movie, none were King Naré Maghann Konaté's brothers). Sundiata's mother, Sogolon Condé, fearing for her son's life, decided to take him to safety. She fled from the kingdom, and King

Sumanguru (acting as Scar in this version) was able to conquer and take the throne.

Much like in the Disney version and in the other variation written above, Sundiata improved himself while in exile. He built alliances, grew as a person, and learned how to lead. The rest is quite the same as the other narrative. He built his private army and battled King Sumanguru in the decisive Battle of Kirina, which won him the kingdom. Though Disney's *The Lion King* is often said to be based on Shakespeare's *Hamlet*, it is hard to deny the similarities between the film and Sundiata's story, especially considering Sundiata was known as the "Lion King." Of course, it is very unlikely that Shakespeare had knowledge of this variation of Sundiata's history when writing *Hamlet*, especially considering how little is known about African history even today. Nonetheless, the parallels are quite incredible.

The Formation of the Mali Empire

Following the intense Battle of Kirina, the remaining Malinké soldiers returned to Sundiata's birth city of Niani, which became the heart and capital of the newly forming Mali Empire. Niani, right on the border of current-day Mali and Guinea, was conveniently located in not only the very fertile Niger Valley but also right in between the Sankarani and Niger Rivers. With Niani as the center of the Mali Empire, the city's people could easily grow more than enough food for themselves, so much so that they began trading and selling food to other towns within their empire and even other kingdoms. Since northern Africa often suffered from droughts, forcing them to source their food from elsewhere, the people of Niani were able to develop a successful, stable economy.

The people of other kingdoms and states, notably that of the fallen Ghana Empire or the Tuareg people, were limited in trading, as transport could only be done on foot, usually by animals. However, those in Niani were able to use their proximity to the river to their advantage. Not only could they get around faster by boat, but merchants from Niani could also transport far more goods by boat than those traveling by horse, camel, or donkey. Although Niani was likely only chosen as the capital city of the Mali Empire because it was the birthplace of its founder, Niani's fertile soils and proximity to the rivers propelled the growth and success of the budding Mali Empire.

Although King Sundiata, unlike his predecessor, was not known for conquering, in 1240, he seized the city of Kumbi, essentially putting an end to the Ghana Empire. The Mali Empire was already prospering due to its agricultural exploits, but by seizing what remained of the Ghana Empire, Sundiata also gained their salt and gold resources, which further drove the newly formed empire's growth. Sundiata was well respected by much of western Africa, and he quickly united the states extending east of Niani all the way to the Atlantic coast. Various Malinké kingdoms along the Niger River were also consolidated into the Mali Empire. Before long, the Mali Empire included not only most of modern-day Mali but also much of the countries surrounding Mali. By accumulating new territories, the Mali Empire gained more goldfields, salt mines, and agricultural resources, as well as large trading cities such as Timbuktu.

On top of its newly acquired resources and already established agricultural exports, the Mali Empire grew economically in other ways. During the 13th century, it was typical to pledge allegiance to one's king and empire by "sacrificing" or gifting various donations, from weapons to food. In addition to the massive profits the Mali Empire made from trade alone, the empire collected taxes on everything that was traded. If something was traded in the Mali Empire, it was taxed. If a merchant had to travel through the Mali Empire to trade something, it was taxed. If the Mali Empire traded something with another kingdom, state, or country, it was taxed. Furthermore, there were many rules on trade; for example, all gold, which was often used almost like currency (until the introduction of cowrie shells), belonged entirely to King Sundiata. That being said, gold dust could legally be traded. Of course, the Mali Empire and its king became extremely wealthy.

Although much had changed from the years when Sundiata was living in exile, Sundiata, the "Lion King," maintained strong leadership, respect, and a powerful army throughout his entire rule. Under Sundiata, kings in the Mali Empire became known as mansa, and the first mansa of the empire did more than just rename the monarch's title. He named generals and officers and rebuilt the royal family by having many kids of his own. He also built up a strong entourage and army. He could rest safely in the knowledge that, even if he was preoccupied, the empire would be led in the right direction and deter the surrounding kingdoms or states from challenging it.

While there is some debate as to Sundiata's religion, it is believed that he converted to Islam at some point during his reign. At this time, almost all of Sundiata's people were Muslim, much like the city of Timbuktu, which would become a part of the Mali Empire. Since a majority of the merchants in the Mali Empire were Muslim themselves, Sundiata's conversion would have boded well politically. And considering he did not force his non-Muslim population to convert, he remained in the public's favor.

Although historians know very little about Sundiata's rule, he established systems that would inspire all of the future leaders of the Mali Empire. While it is hard to say what customs, laws, and systems he introduced himself and which were adapted from previous kings or adopted by his successors, it is without a doubt that elements of Sundiata's reign can be found in the political, economic, and social systems of West Africa and, more specifically, the Mali Empire for centuries after his death.

Chapter 3 – The Subsequent Monarchs of the Mali Empire (1255–1312)

Mansa Uli I

King Sundiata passed away in 1255, and he was succeeded by his son, Uli I. Although Uli was quite young at the time of his father's passing, his exact age is unknown. However, it was believed he was too young to begin reigning as king of the Mali Empire. Until he reached the appropriate age, the empire was supposed to go to one of Sundiata's relatives, Manding Bory (Abubakari I). However, despite his youth, Uli I was ambitious, and he succeeded his father immediately after his death.

Not much is known about the second mansa's reign. It is said that King Uli I helped to expand the Mali Empire's agricultural exploits. Like his father, Uli was Muslim, and at some point in his life, he made the hajj (the pilgrimage/journey to Mecca, Islam's holiest place, located in Saudi Arabia). The custom of taking the hajj is still followed by Muslims today.

Mansa Wati (Ouati)

Although Mansa Uli I's exact dates of birth, death, and reign are not known, it is believed that he died rather suddenly and at a young age. While Sundiata did have other kids, Uli was said to be his only son. And seeing as Uli did not have the chance to have any children, the next heir to the throne was not apparent. That being said, during his reign, Mansa Sundiata adopted at least two boys, Wati and Khalifa, who were children of Malinké generals. The two brothers fought for the throne, and Wati became the first of the two to reign. However, his time in power is seldom mentioned, so little is known about it.

Mansa Khalifa

Though historians are unsure as to why Mansa Wati's reign was only around four years, the throne was passed onto his brother, Khalifa. Mansa Khalifa's rule would be even shorter than his brother's. It is estimated he only spent one year or so on the throne. Nevertheless, he managed to develop quite a negative reputation. Khalifa was said to be quite a cruel leader and apparently shot arrows at his people at random. Within less than a year, the people of the Mali Empire decided to take him off the throne, and he was succeeded by Manding Bory (Abubakari I).

Mansa Manding Bory (Abubakari I or Abu Bakr)

When Sundiata died, the throne was supposed to go to Manding Bory. There was some debate as to who would receive the throne after Uli I, with some suggesting Manding Bory. Yet, despite the numerous times that Manding Bory was considered for the throne, it would not be until Mansa Khalifa was ousted by the people that he would officially take control.

Sundiata was said to have had both a brother and an adopted son named Manding Bory, so it is debated exactly how they were related. However, it is for certain he was related in some way to the first mansa of the Mali Empire. It is more commonly accepted that he was Sundiata's brother; therefore, he was the uncle of the two previous mansas.

Much like his predecessors, little is actually known about Manding Bory's time as the king. Yet he was, without a doubt, far better at his position than his nephews. In his short time as the king, it is believed that he helped save the Mali Empire, which was suffering following the death of Sundiata. During Manding Bory's reign, he helped to not only stabilize the political system but also repair the economy, which was suffering due to the overspending of its previous leaders.

Mansa Sakoura (Sakura)

Unlike all of the previous kings, the sixth mansa of the Mali Empire was not of royal blood, nor was he related to Sundiata. Mansa Sakoura was actually born a slave. However, in the Mali Empire and much of West Africa, being a slave was not necessarily a life sentence, as there was potential for moving up in society. Of course, as with most of the history of the Mali Empire, many of the details are debated, and it is often questioned whether Sakoura was truly a slave or just of a lower or non-royal class. Since all early African history was told orally through very long epic stories that were made easier to remember by including exaggerations, rhyming, or other techniques, it is possible that over the generations, Sakoura's non-royal blood transitioned into him being a slave, making for a more interesting story.

Before becoming the king, Sakoura served as a general in the Mali Empire's army, which would have allowed him to gain attention, favor, and experience from his lower-class position. Since a (likely) former slave was able to ascend the throne, it is believed that the kings and the ruling class of Mali might have had less sway than that of the officers of the court and military generals.

Another fact that is often debated about Sakoura's history is how exactly he managed to ascend to the throne. Some historians believe he was actually the main driver in Mansa Khalifa's removal from the throne, while others claim that he had a thorough and somewhat devious plan for acquiring the throne that allowed him to succeed Manding Bory. Regardless of how he managed to become king, little is known for sure about Mansa Sakoura's reign. Still, he maintained a far better reputation than some of his predecessors.

Mansa Sakoura is said to have greatly expanded the Mali Empire's borders, although historians are not exactly sure what territory he acquired during his reign. While it is heavily debated, some experts claim it was Sakoura who acquired Gao in eastern Mali and extended the empire's territory officially westward to the ocean. Through the various expansions of the Mali Empire, trade and the economy are said to have grown exponentially and thrived in a way it hadn't since its first mansa.

Similar to the Mali Empire's first king, Sundiata, Sakoura was a faithful Muslim and even completed the hajj to Mecca. He reached Mecca safely, but he was not as fortunate on his trip home, as he was killed in the city of Tadjoura. Assuming Sakoura was traveling back from Mecca through Yemen, it would mean he was killed soon after he reentered Africa. While historians are not exactly sure why he was killed, it is often believed it was an armed robbery.

Though historians know more about Mansa Sakoura than his predecessors, this is not due to the oral histories, which seem to specifically leave him out. While Sakoura's reign was extremely favorable to the Mali Empire, his non-royal blood and possible controversial way of achieving the throne is what was mostly spoken about. In the oral histories, he is often referred to as a usurper of the throne. Although Sakoura was a former slave, he is still considered to be a member of the Keita lineage, which means the original Keita dynasty continued uninterrupted even during his reign.

Mansa Gao (Qu)

When the news of Sakoura's death reached the Mali Empire, the reactions were quite mixed. Nevertheless, the former mansa is said to have been buried no differently than if he was a blood relative to the noble family. The Mali Empire and its ruling class did not want another usurper to take the throne after Sakoura, which made the decision for who would succeed him rather difficult. Finally, it was decided that Gao, who is said to have been the nephew of Sundiata, would take the throne.

As with most of the Mali Empire's early history, much is debated, and little is known for sure. While it is certain that Gao was a blood relative of Sundiata, his actual relationship to the first mansa is debated, as it may make more sense for him to be another generation away from Sundiata. It is estimated that Mansa Gao would have begun his reign sometime around the start of the 14th century. While his reign was short-lived, likely only lasting a couple of years, his rule was still an important symbol of the Keita family's influence and the necessity of having a rightful heir to the throne.

Mansa Mohammed ibn Gao (Mohammed ibn Qu)

Mansa Gao's reign was short. If he really was a nephew of Mansa Sundiata, who passed away around 1255 himself, that would have made Gao quite old during his reign, making an early death a likely possibility. Regardless of why his reign only lasted a few (likely around five) years, Mansa Gao was succeeded by his son, Mohammed ibn Gao. Mansa Mohammed ibn Gao's reign is said to have lasted around five years as well. Despite ruling for a short time, the two mansas managed to reign without any major external or internal conflicts or issues, allowing the empire to regain its stability and flourish economically and socially. Mansa Gao and Mansa Mohammed ibn Gao would lead the Mali Empire into its peak period, which began with Mohammed ibn Gao's successor.

The Mali Empire during the Reigns of Mansa Uli I to Mansa Mohammed ibn Gao

The Mali Empire's economy prospered due to its gold and salt mines, two resources that were acquired by Mansa Sundiata when he conquered the Ghana Empire. Both industries were expanded by the subsequent kings. By the 1300s, almost half of the world's gold was actually sourced from gold mines in the Mali Empire. Since the gold trade was closely monitored and run by the kings, salt was, in a way, more valuable to the citizens and even used as currency in the Mali Empire and the sub-Saharan region. While gold still held an almost equal value to salt in North Africa, in the south, where salt was rare but a fundamental part of the people's diet, salt was worth far more than gold.

The Mali Empire truly prospered because of its trade, especially with external regions. Salt, which was abundant in the north, was traded with the southern regions of Africa, and just like gold, all of the salt that passed in or out of the Mali Empire was heavily taxed, increasing the empire's wealth exponentially. Copper, which was also common in the Mali Empire, was another major export.

Over the course of the 12th and 13th centuries, the Mali Empire continued to build up its military presence, turning its armed forces into what would become known as the "Malinké war machine." Regardless of who was in charge, the empire depended on conscription, which required every tribe and region within the empire to give a certain quota of soldiers. This was necessary, as the empire's borders were constantly being defended in order to not only tax merchants coming in or leaving the Mali Empire but also to protect the citizens against possible threats. It is estimated that at any given time in the late 12th and early 13th century, the empire would have had an active military of around 100,000 soldiers.

Since the Mali Empire's army was incredibly powerful and more than unlikely unmatched by any other military nearby at the time, the Mali Empire continued to slowly conquer land and expand its borders. Eventually, the Mali Empire became too large for one single army, and the military was essentially split in half, although they were all still governed by the reigning mansa. The empire's military was separated into the northern army, whose commander, or *farin*, was stationed in Soura, and the southern army, whose commander, or *sankar*, was stationed in Zouma. While most men fought on foot with shields and spears or bows, the higher-ranked members of the military would be given horses and more powerful weapons. The cavalry, which totaled around ten thousand men, were given poison-tipped or flaming arrows, as well as swords, lances, chain mail armor, and even javelins laced with poison.

Mansa Abubakari II

There is some debate as to whether or not Mansa Mohammed ibn Gao was the direct predecessor to Mansa Musa or whether Mansa Abubakari II followed Mansa Mohammed Ibn Gao. Abubakari II, who was also known as Bata Manding Bory, is said to have been a relative, perhaps the son, of the fifth mansa of the Mali Empire, Manding Bory (Abubakari I). While dates are quite difficult to confirm in the early years of the Mali Empire, it is thought that Mansa Abubakari II took the throne around 1310.

According to his successor, Mansa Abubakari II was far more interested in the Western world than his own empire and sent two expeditions west. The king actually embarked on the second journey, and despite his absence, the empire remained stable and continued to flourish. Although Mansa Abubakari II set sail on the second voyage, neither of the ships returned to the Mali Empire. Whether the crew actually survived is highly debated. Some historians believe both expeditions failed and that all the passengers on the ships perished at sea. Others think that the Mali Empire's eventual favorable relations with the Americas might actually be due to the expeditions' success. Some people even believe that the Mali Empire beat Spain's famous voyages, led by Christopher Columbus, reaching the Americas more than 150 years before. However, this has yet to be proven. Regardless of whether the expeditions were successful in reaching the Americas or not, Mansa Abubakari II never returned to the Mali Empire and thus abdicated the throne.

Chapter 4 – Mansa Musa (1312–1337)

Mansa Musa's Ascension to the Throne

Before one can begin discussing Mansa Musa himself or his effect on the Mali Empire and the city of Timbuktu, it is important to discuss his accession to the throne. His relations to the previous kings and his actual accession to the throne are somewhat controversial. And this is on top of the fact that Musa brought about a change in the lineage. Up to this point in history, Mansa Sundiata, the creator of the Mali Empire, was by far the most well-known emperor. However, the tenth mansa would make a name for himself unlike anyone who reigned before him and debatably unlike any other leader on the entire continent up until that point in history.

Musa is said to have begun his reign around 1312, and he is not known by the modern world for his policies, advancements, or life but rather for his wealth. Of course, as with much of the Mali Empire's early history, Mansa Musa's wealth and entire life are debated. Most of what we know about Mali's tenth emperor comes from oral sources or ancient historians from other countries who briefly met the king or, more likely, met those who met the king.

Historians are almost certain that Mansa Musa was a grandson or at least a direct relative to the fifth mansa of the Mali Empire, Mansa Manding Bory (Abubakari I). This is why Musa's predecessor's lineage is heavily debated. Abubakari II is believed to have been the son of Abubakari I, but most historians do not believe he was the father to Mansa Musa. This could mean that Mansa Musa's predecessor was his uncle or his father's cousin. But since nothing is known about Abubakari I or II's family, Mansa Musa's and his predecessor's relation is not known for sure.

Mansa Musa's father is known as Faga Laye, who is said to have had no real impact on the Mali Empire's history other than raising the empire's most famous king. Why Faga Laye was never mansa is unknown, but it is possible he died before the throne was available. Either way, with the accession of Mansa Musa to the throne, a new lineage began: the Laye lineage. Of course, even though Mansa Musa marked the beginning of a new lineage for the Mali Empire, the throne still never truly passed out of the first dynasty's hands, as Musa was somehow related to the first mansa of the Mali Empire, Sundiata. Though nine mansas had followed in between Sundiata's and Musa's reign, they would remain the two most well-known kings of the Mali Empire. Fittingly, Musa not only shared his acclaim with his great uncle but also his nickname. Mansa Musa also became known as the Lion of Mali.

It is said that Musa served briefly as the deputy to his predecessor. When Abubakari II left on his voyage, Musa acted as a regent, filling in while his predecessor explored the unknown world. As recounted above, Abubakari II did not return from his expedition, and Musa simply continued ruling and was officially named mansa. Since everything worked out very conveniently for Musa, some historians speculate that there may have been some foul play involved. The only source of what happened to Abubakari II comes from Mansa Musa himself, which leads some to believe that Musa's predecessor was not really a victim of the sea but perhaps a victim of his successor. Historians are unsure whether Abubakari II's voyage is just a cover-up story or if he truly did set off out west but was then targeted by Musa soon after his departure. Either way, it is commonly believed that Musa might have acquired the title of mansa through dishonest means.

The Mali Empire at the Time of Mansa Musa's Rise to the Throne

While Mansa Musa certainly helped to expand the Mali Empire and grow its wealth, he inherited a large portion of his wealth, as well as territories used for making money. With the vague oral histories of the Mali Empire, it is not known for sure what land was acquired by which king, but by the time Musa became the mansa, the Mali Empire had five major cities: Niani, Koumbi Saleh, Gao, Jenne, and, of course, Timbuktu. The latter may have been acquired by Musa himself, but even if it wasn't, Mansa Musa was the one who turned Timbuktu into a major hub.

The Mali Empire's capital city, Niani, which was the birthplace of the Mali Empire's creator, was at its peak during the time of Mansa Musa's reign. Niani served as the political, economic, and social hub of the empire, though the other cities, specifically Timbuktu, were growing exponentially and catching up with the capital city.

Similar to the previous mansas, Mansa Musa had inherited rapidly growing gold and salt industries, which could easily provide more than enough funds for the developing empire. However, during Mansa Musa's reign, newer industries were beginning to form, such as slavery and different types of crops, like the kola nut, which would help to exponentially grow the Mali Empire and, of course, Mansa Musa's wealth. This was especially true in the city of Gao, which served as the ideal trading center for slaves across the Sahara Desert.

Since Mali was perfectly located around the fertile Niger River, the empire had unparalleled growing seasons, which allowed agricultural exports to be worth investing in, almost as much as gold or salt. Food was in high demand in the drier regions of Africa, especially sorghum, millet, and rice which was extremely scarce across the continent.

The five major cities of the Mali Empire formed the trans-Saharan trade routes, which are still recognized today as one of the most fundamental trade routes of classical society. Just as the previous mansas had done, Musa implemented strict taxation upon all those who crossed through the Mali Empire. And seeing as the trans-Saharan routes went through the Mali Empire and many of its large cities, it is no surprise that Musa is considered to be one of the wealthiest men in history.

By the time of Musa's reign, trading hubs had already been established all over Africa, with many of the largest ones being located in the Mali Empire itself. Timbuktu became known as an important stop for merchants from Egypt, who either traveled back and forth between the two places or used Timbuktu as a layover spot before continuing along the trans-Saharan routes.

While the economy was certainly a major reason for travel between regions, trading hubs could not and would not attract as many people to travel as religion. By this time, most of the Mali Empire and its surrounding territories were Muslim. Thus, embarking on the hajj was commonplace. Mecca, which was the holiest place to the people in the Mali Empire, is said to be the birthplace of the Prophet Muhammad, and it attracted tens of thousands of people every year during Musa's reign. Any Muslim located in West Africa had to travel through the Mali Empire, where they were, of course, taxed for entering. The trip, which took many months on camelback, remains an important part of Islam; today, approximately two million people a year make the journey to Mecca.

When Mansa Musa inherited the throne, most of his subjects were Muslim, yet not all of them could travel to Mecca every year for the hajj. As a result, cities within the Mali Empire started to become individual religious hubs. The city of Jenne (also known as Djenné), located between the Niger and Bani Rivers, grew due to the trade routes. Jenne specifically had the benefit of being located right near the border of the empire, making it conveniently accessible from Sudan and Guinea. However, despite Jenne being a convenient location for trade, it would not become known for being a trading hub like Niani; instead, it was known as a religious hub. Under Mansa Musa, Jenne would become known as one of the Mali Empire's centers for Muslim learning.

Timbuktu at the Time of Mansa Musa's Accession to the Throne

By the time Musa became the mansa, Timbuktu had already earned a similar reputation as both Niani and Jenne. It became known as a conglomerate for both trading and religious affairs, and this reputation brought travelers and settlers from surrounding regions. Around the start of the 14th century, the population of Timbuktu was said to be around ten thousand or more. Of course, its population is speculative, and it is possible that the estimations of ancient populations are off. Regardless of the exact number of people in Timbuktu at the time, when Mansa Musa took his throne, Timbuktu was already an urban hub. It attracted visitors and settlers from all over the world, but its growth was only just beginning.

Mansa Musa I

Wealth

While all of the previous kings of the Mali Empire had successfully taken advantage of the gold mines in their territory, none did so like Mansa Musa. Unlike his predecessors, he did not simply enjoy the riches of the mines but also realized the importance of the industry. Musa invested heavily in expanding mining, which helped to grow his finances exponentially.

Mansa Musa's wealth is often described as being, well, indescribable. Imagine a stereotypical wealthy cartoon king sitting in a room surrounded by all of the gold in the world; now, double the amount of gold, and you have a better idea of Musa's wealth. In fact, at the time of his reign, it is estimated that Mansa Musa had around half of all of the mined gold in the world. The rest of it was likely split between other Old World rulers, which means that Musa would have had the largest collection of gold in the world.

In addition to his personal collection of gold and his territory's gold mines and deposits, the Mali Empire had some of the largest gold trading centers in the world at the time. And like all products in the Mali Empire, gold was heavily taxed when traded. According to the laws that had been established by Musa's predecessors, all the gold in the Mali Empire actually belonged to the mansa, so even gold not in his personal collection can technically be added to his riches. To increase the mansa's gold revenues, any merchant who traveled through the Mali Empire paid a duty. Since Mali's cities had some of the best gold trading posts, anyone looking to purchase gold was taxed upon entering the empire, earning the king money even if they didn't buy gold at all. This meant that the emperor earned revenue from every single step in the gold mining process, from the mining and exporting to trading and traveling. And all of this on top of the gold he actually kept for himself.

Though Mansa Musa is known for his gold, the Mali Empire had many other industries at the time. Mansa Musa inherited the same industries and resources as his predecessors, notably salt, copper, and agriculture, which he helped to develop on a large scale. Markets were also beginning to pop up, and global trade grew, bringing in profits on products that used to have little demand. One example of this was ivory. Ivory had always been popular, but the industry rapidly grew since foreign merchants began seeking the product, which was rare outside of Africa. Luckily for the Mali

Empire, elephants and hippopotamuses, whose tusks are the main sources of ivory, were extremely common at the time, though this is not the case anymore, specifically because of this growing demand.

The increase of global trade not only catapulted new industries in the Mali Empire but also drastically increased the demand for its already existing products. While Mansa Musa certainly helped to increase his own wealth by investing in industries, building "attractions" (mostly religious ones) for travelers, and spreading the word of his empire's products and riches, most of his riches can be attributed to timing. The 1300s marked the start of a more globally intertwined society and market. While it would be many more centuries until the world would reach the true beginning of a global economy, the 14th century certainly brought the continents closer together, as merchants traveled to trading hubs, diplomats and royal leaders met to discuss foreign relations, and countries embarked on expeditions and engaged in a race for colonization. This is not to downplay Mansa Musa's financial sense when it came to expanding his industries. However, had he been on the throne in the previous decades, he likely would not have been considered one of the richest men in history, as his economic growth would not have been possible in the same way.

Religion

Though the Mali Empire was certainly worth paying attention to in the 1300s, the world did not suddenly gain knowledge of its existence as soon as Mansa Musa took the throne. In fact, it would be his hajj that would put him and his territory on the map. Of course, Mansa Musa was not the first emperor to engage in this ancient Islamic pilgrimage, as at least two of his predecessors had also taken part in the tradition. That being said, no mansa of the Mali Empire would be better known for his hajj than Musa.

While the date is not known for sure, it is estimated that Mansa Musa would have left on his pilgrimage around 1324, so a little more than a decade after he took the throne. The mansa's hajj began in Niani, which should come as no surprise since this was the Mali Empire's capital city. As mansa, Musa did not leave alone; he was accompanied by tens of thousands of men and likely some women as well. In total, an estimated sixty thousand people made the journey. Among those caravans, which were all dressed in Persian silk and brocade, there were around twelve thousand slaves.

Though many of the king's Muslim subjects would have wished for nothing more than to accompany the mansa on his journey to Mecca, the reason for his large entourage was one of necessity. Some of the tens of thousands of people who accompanied him were security, which was important, especially considering that Mansa Sakoura had been murdered on his pilgrimage. However, that being said, most of the people traveling with Musa were there to help transport and guard the incredible amount of gold and wealth he was bringing on the journey. On top of the gold-adorned staff that each slave in front of him carried to immediately convey the king's wealth, Mansa Musa was followed by around eighty camels which each carried three hundred pounds of gold. Altogether, he brought around twenty-four thousand pounds of gold with him on the journey. This was not done just to boast or make the king look good but to strategically inform the surrounding territories of the Mali Empire's riches.

Of course, with that being said, carrying around tens of thousands of pounds of gold on a long journey is sure to be an ego boost. As the mansa made his way to Mecca, Saudi Arabia, every region he passed took notice of the king, his gold, and his entourage. Mansa Musa and his posse passed through Egypt, and when he stopped in Cairo, he was invited to meet Sultan al-Malik al-Nasir. Though Musa first turned down the offer, as he did not want to formally greet the ruler of Cairo since it would entail kissing the ground at the sultan's feet, Musa eventually agreed to meet al-Malik al-Nasir. The sultan agreed to house Mansa Musa and his entire entourage during his stay in Cairo.

In return, Mansa Musa gave away thousands of pounds of gold, which was a rare commodity in Cairo at the time. The Mali emperor is said to have given gold to royal officers, diplomats, and impoverished civilians. In fact, some say he even littered the streets with gold. This made quite an impact, especially on Egypt's economy, which experienced insane inflation due to the increase of gold. Supposedly, it took around twelve years for the country to recover financially from Musa's visit. Of course, Mansa Musa's actions were well-intentioned, and despite his negative impact on the economy, the people of Egypt loved Musa. This affection was also shared by the country's royalty as well.

After Egypt, Mansa Musa traveled through the Middle Eastern regions, where his well-dressed entourage and extreme generosity were noticed and admired. Though Mansa Musa's hajj would end up being one of the best advertising schemes in history, it is believed by historians that his actions were no scheme at all but simply Musa being himself. Regardless of his original intentions, word of his pilgrimage spread around Africa, the Middle East, and eventually Europe. Years after his death, Mansa Musa was depicted sitting on a throne holding a gold scepter and gold nugget and wearing a crown on the 1375 Catalan Atlas, created by famous Spanish cartographer Abraham Cresques. This atlas was an important tool for medieval European navigators. This means much of Europe would have heard of Mansa Musa and the Mali Empire by the end of the 14th century.

While Musa's hajj put him and his empire on the map, historians believe that, for him, it was still about religion. After months of travel, Musa would eventually make it to Mecca, which would fuel his interest in spreading his religious beliefs. Upon returning home, Mansa Musa began transforming the Mali Empire by gradually commissioning architects, scholars, and engineers to build Islamic educational buildings and mosques. Though the Mali

Empire was already Muslim and had many impressive buildings displaying its devotion to the religion, Musa would commission some of the most well-known structures of the Mali Empire. Some of these well-known buildings include Sankoré Madrasah, the Djinguereber or Great Mosque, and the Madugu royal residence. Since so many great scholars and artists had actually followed Mansa Musa back from his hajj, he had plenty of knowledgeable men to design, build, and teach in his new institutions.

Inhabitants of the Mali Empire now had many places to choose from for Friday prayers. And due to the increase in Islamic libraries, schools, and monuments, the Mali Empire began attracting Muslims from all over the world. Religion transformed the Mali Empire into a diverse, multilingual nation unlike other kingdoms in Africa or even the world at the time. Religion had more of an impact on the empire than trade.

This was especially true in Timbuktu, which became known as the true heart of Islamic studies in the Mali Empire. This was due to the construction of the University of Sankoré, which had more than twenty thousand students enrolled at any given time after opening. This was in addition to the Islamic library in Timbuktu, which became undoubtedly the best library for not only Islamic resources but also all studies in the whole of Africa. After the opening of the University of Sankoré, Timbuktu would attract Muslim scholars from other regions in Africa, the Middle East, Asia, and Europe. Although the school's focus was on religion, students could also learn math, law, science, literature, and grammar.

Before Mansa Musa's reign, books were somewhat rare in the Mali Empire, but the well-off leader invested in high-quality paper from China. Before long, a new industry would begin in the Mali Empire: the book industry. By the end of Musa's life, books became the most valuable product in all of the Mali Empire. For those who could not afford to buy or invest in books, citizens had access to some of the most advanced libraries of that age. It is estimated that at that time, the Mali Empire's many libraries housed approximately 400,000 books and manuscripts. By 1400, Sankoré Madrasah alone was said to house around 700,000 books.

Timbuktu would also be home to the Djinguereber Mosque, which was another well-known learning and religious center. It attracted thousands of Islamic students. Built in 1327, the Djinguereber Mosque remained active for nearly five hundred years and is still standing today. According to reports, Mansa Musa actually commissioned Abu Es Haq es Saheli, an architect born in Spain, to design the mosque for over four hundred pounds of gold.

While Mansa Musa was not the first Muslim leader of the Mali Empire, he certainly was the most devoted, at least as far as the records are aware. Similar to his predecessors, Musa did not try to force the Mali Empire's diverse population into converting to Islam, although he did attempt to make it the official religion of the royal family and administration. Though much of the population was Muslim, there were many acquired territories that had already established their own native tribal religions. Furthermore, the kingdom had many settlers from elsewhere, so forcing the population to convert would have certainly resulted in many rebellions. Yet, despite not forcing his population to convert, Mansa Musa would remain devoted to his faith. In addition to completing the hajj and building many religious structures in his empire, he also made the Eid celebrations, which mark the end of fasting and take place at the end of Ramadan, official national celebrations. On top of commissioning the construction of many Islamic educational institutions, Mansa Musa was said to have been a lifelong student, as he learned to read and write in Arabic.

Politics

While Mansa Musa is recognized today for his wealth and his influence on Islamic culture in Africa, he was still an extremely intelligent leader. This is, of course, apparent in his expansion of the Mali Empire's industries and his fantastic yet accidental foreign relations tour while on the hajj. However, as emperor, he did play a large role in the politics of the Mali Empire, and he introduced many new policies, systems, and territories to the empire.

While it is debated what was brought into the kingdom by each mansa, Musa is credited with bringing a lot of change to the Mali Empire. For example, the Mali Empire already had a pretty impressive military by the time Mansa Musa ascended the throne. But with the empire rapidly growing, it was important that the military grew at a similar pace. Musa knew the necessity of a large and efficient army. While it never had to defend the empire from any real threats during his reign, the Mali Empire's army was crucial in policing the trans-Saharan trade routes, which crossed through the empire's territory. The military also controlled small internal rebellions and dissuaded any external attacks.

Another important reason Mansa Musa cared so much about growing his army is that he was focused on growing his empire's territory. As mentioned many times in this book, it is not known which territory was brought in by which mansa; some historians even believe that Timbuktu was not a part of the Mali Empire until Mansa Musa's reign, while others cite it as being included in the empire for decades before him. Yet, there are some acquisitions that are not debated at all. While on the hajj, Mansa Musa was quite busy, keeping track of thousands of people, visiting with surrounding regions' monarchs, fulfilling his religious tasks, handing out gold, and conquering the territory of Gao for the Mali Empire. Of course, it is more than likely that it was not actually Mansa Musa himself who acquired the region but one of his generals. This general would have scouted the land, informed the king, and returned and conquered the land with the ruler's permission.

Regardless of how it was acquired exactly, Mansa Musa managed to obtain Gao, which had belonged to the Songhai state. He also added hundreds of miles of land to the Mali Empire. By the end of Musa's reign, the Mali Empire was, without exaggeration, one of the largest empires in the world during that century. It included, of course, modern-day Mali, as well as modern-day Guinea, Nigeria, Niger, Senegal, Gambia, Chad, and Mauritania. According to travelers of that era, it would take around four months to traverse just from the empire's northern border to Niani, which wasn't even the southernmost city. According to some reports from the time, it took around one year to traverse the Mali Empire from its eastern border to its western border. This calculation would have taken into account challenges, such as traversing rivers, deserts, and other difficult stretches of land, which would be much easier to cross with modern technology.

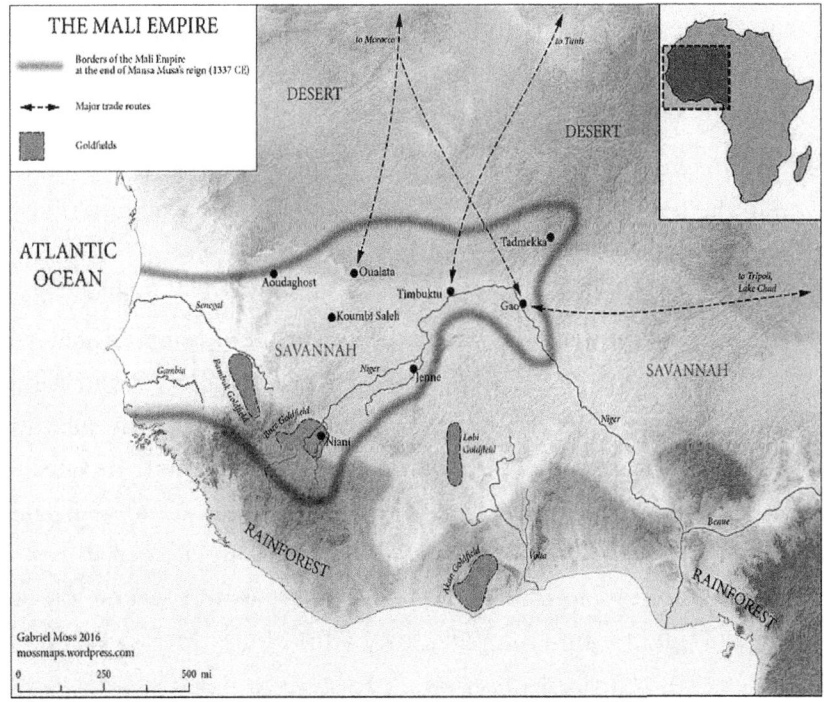

The extent of the Mali Empire at the end of Mansa Musa's reign
Gabriel Moss, CC BY-SA 4.0 <https://creativecommons.org/licenses/by-sa/4.0>, via Wikimedia Commons https://commons.wikimedia.org/wiki/File:The_Mali_Empire.jpg

Gao

Once Mansa Musa returned back to his kingdom, rather than heading straight to his residence in Niani or any of his other previously established cities, he visited Gao. Much like Timbuktu or Niani, Gao was an ancient city that had been established centuries before it was acquired by the Mali Empire. Gao is said to have been founded as early as the 7th century. In fact, it was one of the oldest trading cities in the entire western region of Africa.

Sometime in the 1000s, the Gao region was acquired by the Songhai state, and it became its capital city, as well as a hub for the gold, slave, salt, and copper trade, much like the Mali Empire's own respective trading cities. Seeing as it had been the heart of the Songhai state's operations for over three hundred years, the region was already established with buildings, mosques, and trading centers when Mansa Musa acquired the land in 1325.

Though Mansa Musa's general may have conquered the land for the empire during the emperor's hajj, the region's previous king still lived in the territory. So, when Musa visited his newly acquired land, he had to pay the Songhai monarch a visit. While in Gao, Musa demanded and received submission from the Songhai state's previous king and took his sons as captives. The Songhai state did not entirely dissipate after that meeting, but it would remain within the Mali Empire's dominion with very little power for the next few decades. Of course, the population of Gao was quite dissatisfied with the change of government, and they would continuously stage small rebellions throughout the 14th century in an attempt to regain control of the region. The Songhai state would eventually be successful, but not until many decades after Mansa Musa's death.

Finally, after his long pilgrimage that went on for nearly, if not an entire year, Mansa Musa returned home to Niani, where he began commissioning architects to build incredible mosques and Islamic education centers all over his empire, specifically in the cities of

Timbuktu and Gao. While Gao already had many famous monuments built by its previous owners, Mansa Musa would commission some iconic structures, most of which were religious. They were built out of burnt bricks, which was a new construction method introduced in Africa at the time.

Other Acquired Lands and Administration

Over the course of Musa's reign, he acquired more land and continued to expand the Mali Empire's borders. By the end of his reign, the Mali Empire included more than four hundred unique and diverse towns, villages, and cities. It is said that the only empire in the world that was larger at the time was the Mongol Empire, meaning that the Mali Empire was by far the largest African empire.

This expansion of land required a change in the divisions of the empire, and while it is not often spoken about, changes in the Mali Empire's divisions were certainly one of the most beneficial adjustments made by the tenth mansa. While the Mali Empire was already divided into some smaller regions by the time he ascended to the throne, the territory needed to be broken down into smaller regions in order to run efficiently as Mali's borders continued to expand.

Previously, the empire was divided into three states. However, a few years into Mansa Musa's reign, he realized that this system was no longer working. Musa split the massive Mali Empire into fourteen smaller provinces, which were each run by its own respective governor. The larger populations within each province were officially split into towns and cities, which was led by a mayor.

While Mansa Musa remained the supreme leader of the Mali Empire, his power began to decentralize as his territory grew. Musa and the royal family remained in Niani, and according to reports from the time, the farther a territory was from the capital city, the less influence the mansa had on it. Yet, no matter how far away one found themselves from Niani, if one lived in the Mali Empire, one remained a subject of Mansa Musa. The people were reminded of this control through taxes. Overall, Mansa Musa was respected by much of his population, and rebellions were not very frequent and always manageable.

In every town, city, or village, the military chiefs, or *kun-tiguis*, elected the village leader, sort of like a mayor, who was generally of a well-respected bloodline in that region. This helped to gain the approval of the civilians. Above the local administration was a county leader, which was known as the *kafo-tigui*. *Kafo-tiguis* were generally chosen by the governor of the county's respective province. There was usually some nepotism or favoritism involved in these decisions, as the governor would choose a *kafo-tigui* he already knew and was friends or colleagues with. Much like in modern-day countries, every individual province had its own unique government that was run separately from the supreme leader. Some provinces used more modern election formats, while others simply used lineage or inheritance to decide who would control the province. These governors of the province were known as *dyamani-tigui*, and while they could be appointed as the province saw fit, they had to be approved by the mansa to officially take the position.

If the mansa did not approve of the province's self-appointed *dyamani-tigui*, he would likely appoint a trustworthy *farba* until another candidate could be chosen. A *farba* was specifically picked by the mansa, and he would take on the typical duties of a political leader, either in order to replace or oversee a region's administration. Since Mansa Musa had little influence over his many provinces, he often appointed a *farba*, who simply acted as a safeguard, connecting him to the far-away regions and ensuring that the province's administration was still respecting his wishes. The position of *farba* was often given to members of the royal family. However, respected slaves could also earn the position, and once they earned it, they could expect their children to replace them one day, continuing the administrative lineage in that province. While the *farba* often would work in tandem with the local government, aiding in the running of the province and reporting back to the mansa, the *farba* had the right to remove any political figure, control the province's army, and take over the government if necessary.

While Mansa Musa had created quite an impressive political system, the use of *farbas* and *farins* was often a necessity to keep order in the massive empire. *Farins* were similar to *farbas*, but rather than always being posted in a province to oversee the local government, they were often used to temporarily run a government following the new acquisition of territory. The *farin* would have to understand how to introduce the new taxes, help arrange a new government, control a dissatisfied population, and get citizens to submit to their new king after the territory was conquered. The position of *farin* required someone who understood politics, people, and how to gracefully transition a population to being part of the Mali Empire. After a suitable amount of time had passed, and as long as the *farin* felt that a population was ready, the province could elect its own government. At this point, the *farin's* job was complete.

Mansa Musa's Legacy

Though every mansa of the Mali Empire made a difference in the systems, culture, policies, territory, religion, and beliefs during their reigns, none made as large of an impact as Mansa Musa. Whether it was his grand persona, his intelligent decisions, his timing, his smart financial moves, or his successful foreign relations, something about the tenth mansa of the Mali Empire was different from his predecessors. Despite the fact that he conquered plenty of land during his reign, Mansa Musa was well respected by his subjects, and his reign was unusually smooth. He was even respected by foreign monarchs and regions, which was almost entirely due to his year-long hajj, during which Musa gave away so much gold that he apparently had to take out a loan in order to give it back to the Mali Empire.

Though records show that some people believed Mansa Musa wasted too much money, specifically while on his hajj, there is no doubt that his illustrious, famous journey to Mecca was beneficial for the Mali Empire in the end, as it brought intellectuals and merchants, not to mention respect, from the surrounding regions. Though Musa is often depicted sitting on a pile of gold, Mansa Musa put much of the empire's finances into the cultivation of education, religion, and economy. And although the populations in the lands he conquered may not agree, Musa's spending often resulted in the betterment of his subjects' lives. While he certainly was lavish, this grand persona attracted the attention of many important figures who came to the Mali Empire to meet the mystical king. Mansa Musa used his considerable wealth to bring his empire into the future, advancing his territories into modern society at a far faster rate than any nearby region.

Like any ruler of his time, Mansa Musa was not without his faults, and he could certainly be criticized for outdated beliefs or policies. Yet, he was, without a doubt, one of the most advanced and modern rulers of the 14th century. The focus he put on education, albeit mostly religious education, was unheard of in Africa and even in most of the world during that time. Under his rule, he transformed the Mali Empire into a modern conglomerate, which housed some of the most advanced religious, commercial, and education structures in the world. For centuries after his death, people would travel thousands of miles to visit the state-of-the-art structures he commissioned during his life.

Mansa Musa is said to have died in 1337 at the age of fifty-seven, yet his memory would live on for many years after his death, as he put the Mali Empire on the map. While the Mali Empire would not last for much longer after his death, elements of his reign are still present even today in the political, cultural, and economic organization and systems. Though Timbuktu had been inhabited for centuries before Mansa Musa and had been a trading hub for decades before his reign, he is the reason that people know the city's name today.

The Berber and Tuareg Population during Mansa Musa's Reign

Though Timbuktu and its surrounding areas changed drastically between the 5th century, when it was run by the Tuaregs, and the 14th century, when it was a part of the Mali Empire, its original people remained. The Tuareg people established the region's first trade routes, trade cities, and gold and salt mines. They even helped to establish the Islamic religion before Sundiata had even created the Mali Empire.

As with many native populations around the world, the Tuaregs did not get to maintain control of their land, as the burgeoning kingdoms nearby were quick to assert their authority. That being said, while the Tuaregs were far from satisfied with being forced to be a subject of the Mali Empire, they were still an important asset to the economy, meaning they were not treated as badly as native populations in other parts of the world. After all, the Tuaregs had spent centuries learning how to survive the Sahara Desert, meaning they were the most efficient at traversing the tough landscape, which was necessary for trade at the time.

While many of the Tuareg and Berber populations continued to remain in pockets within the Mali Empire, sticking to their old traditions, others converted to the Mali Empire's way of life. The well-known Ibn Battuta is a perfect example of how the native populations in the Mali Empire and all of Africa evolved with the changing governments. Born in Tangier, Ibn Battuta was extremely well-traveled and eventually made his way to Timbuktu. He documented much of his journeys, which allowed historians to have a better understanding of life in the 14th century. According to Ibn Battuta, during his visit to Timbuktu in 1353, the people were mostly veiled, which is perhaps a reference to the Tuareg population, and the region was run by a governor known as Farba

Musa.

Regardless of what Timbuktu looked like when Ibn Battuta visited, after Mansa Musa returned from his hajj, the city transformed rapidly. As new structures went up and populations flocked to the city, it is very likely that the Tuareg population was pushed out. As little is known about the Mali Empire, even less is known about the Tuareg population at this time, so it is difficult to know exactly how the Tuareg people adapted to living within the Mali Empire. However, considering the rebellions that are still occurring today, it is likely that the native population was not pleased by the changes taking place. All the knowledge we have today of the Tuareg people during the period of the Mali Empire comes from external accounts, such as the vague ones from Ibn Battuta, which makes it hard to decipher the truth. Yet, considering the lack of information in a time when the book industry was making just as much, if not more than gold, we can assume that the Tuareg population that stayed in the Mali Empire either kept to themselves or assimilated.

Chapter 5 – The Mali Empire after Mansa Musa (1337–1360)

Mansa Maghan

Following Mansa Musa's death in 1337, the throne was succeeded by his younger son, Maghan, whose name translates to Muhammad, demonstrating his devotion to Islam. Maghan was actually chosen by his father to be the deputy of the Mali Empire while Musa was on his hajj. Apparently, Mansa Musa, at some point, considered returning to Mecca to settle there permanently. If he had done this, he would have abdicated the throne, with Maghan then stepping in to take over. However, this, of course, did not happen, as Musa ruled over the Mali Empire until his death.

Even though Maghan was not the oldest son, he was chosen as his father's successor because he had been appointed as a deputy by his father and had experience in an administrative role. This was especially fitting, as Mansa Musa had been named a deputy when his predecessor, Abubakari II, embarked on his own journey. Unlike Abubakari II, though, Musa returned home from his travels and held the throne until his death.

Since Mansa Musa had successfully set up the empire, its wealth continued to grow under his son's leadership. That being said, Mansa Maghan was reported to have wasted money, and unlike his father, Maghan's spending brought no benefits to the kingdom. Though there is little known about Mansa Maghan, he does not hold the best reputation as emperor. He is often compared to Mansa Khalifa because they both received negative feedback from the population. Of course, it would have been extremely difficult to follow the beloved Mansa Musa, which may have contributed to Mansa Maghan's poor reception.

Other than the overspending, Maghan is not really known for doing anything else during his reign, which is unsurprising, as he only held the throne for four years.

Mansa Suleyman

Similar to many of the previous mansas of the Mali Empire, Suleyman's exact relation to the lineage is debated, with many historians believing him to be the oldest of Mansa Musa's sons. However, others claim he was Musa's brother. Either way, he was certainly a blood relative of the tenth mansa, and he was older than Mansa Maghan, which means he should have been, in theory, first in line for the throne after the death of Musa. Considering Maghan was rather young when he inherited the throne and died after only being mansa for four years, many historians believe that his successor may have been involved in his death, both because Suleyman wanted faster access to the throne and because he wanted retribution for not being named mansa as the oldest living male relative of Musa. Historians are not alone in their suspicions of Mansa Suleyman, as it seems many people in the Mali Empire doubted his rise to power, which certainly would have cast some doubt on the entire royal family.

Suleyman acquired the throne in 1341, and he would rule as mansa for decades longer than his predecessor. During this time, he caused the people of the Mali Empire to have even less trust and respect for the administration. Similar to the Tuareg people during the 14th century, much of what we know about Mansa Suleyman is from external sources, specifically that of Ibn Battuta.

Ibn Battuta, who was researching for a manuscript he would publish later known as *Travels in Asia and Africa*, spent many months with Mansa Suleyman, observing the king from the inside. According to Ibn Battuta, Suleyman was an extremely strict ruler, especially when it came to money. He rarely spent his wealth in order to help restore the empire's economy after his wasteful predecessor. Though Mansa Suleyman would prove to be successful in fixing the empire's financial situation and was an overall powerful and intelligent leader, he was strict to a fault, which led the population to dislike him. Matters were made worse by the fact that the royal family was divided on who should be the next mansa. The Mali Empire was also starting to outgrow its leadership by the mid-14th century, meaning there were many rebellions.

On top of the family drama, which mostly stemmed from the fact that Musa's son Maghan had passed away after only four years as mansa, with Suleyman being accused as the perpetrator, there was a massive conspiracy within the royal family to overthrow Suleyman during his reign. According to Ibn Battuta, who was actually present for the trials, "It happened during my sojourn in Mali that the Sultan was angry with his chief wife, the daughter of his paternal uncle, named Qasa [Queen.] She is his partner in the kingship...He imprisoned her with one of the chiefs, and raised in her place another wife, Bandju, who was not from the daughters of the kings."

Ibn Battuta continued to explain that Suleyman brought his ex-wife, as well as other members of the royal family, to a sort of trial. During the trial, in the words of Ibn Battuta, "Then a female slave of Qasa was brought in with chains on her hands and legs. She was told to say what she knew. She told that Qasa had sent her to Djatal, a son of the paternal uncle of the Sultan...She invited him to overthrow the Sultan, informing him that she herself and all the armies were ready to accept him as a ruler." According to Ibn Battuta, when the chiefs of the court heard this, they sentenced her to execution. Though Suleyman managed to intercept and prevent the coup d'état that his ex-wife and blood relatives had planned, it would not be the last plot for the throne. Over the following years, tensions would continue to rise within the royal family, and the Mali Empire's administration would remain unstable.

Internal family issues would not be the only difficulties that Mansa Suleyman would face during his reign. Disdain for the administration was gradually rising in the years following the death of Mansa Musa. During Suleyman's time as mansa, this dissatisfaction would be demonstrated through many rebellions. One of the main populations rebelling within the Mali Empire was the Tuaregs, who had lived in the territory for centuries. Much like the newer civilians, the Tuaregs did not favor the current monarch or administration.

Suleyman would also face trouble externally when the Fula people (also known as Fulani people) began raiding Takrur, which was a territory within the Mali Empire. Though Suleyman successfully defended the Mali Empire from the Fula raids, at the same time, the people of the Dyolof province in modern-day Senegal formed their own empire, known as the Jolof Empire. Due to this, the Mali Empire lost a significant chunk of land.

Mansa Suleyman certainly had to deal with far more issues than any of his recent predecessors. Yet, like Mansa Musa, he managed to stay completely devoted to his religious beliefs while on the throne. Suleyman also successfully completed his own hajj, during which he improved relations with foreign monarchs and regions, such as Egypt and Morocco. After visiting Saudi Arabia, he brought back many holy books, which he would eventually place in a building he had commissioned known as Camanbolon, which was also used as a court.

Historians often debate the exact timeline of Mansa Suleyman's accession to the throne, as the chronology of rulers is confusing. Although it is widely thought that Suleyman ruled for twenty-four years and Mansa Maghan ruled for four, it is often believed that Mansa Musa ruled until his death in 1337. This makes no sense chronologically because we know that Suleyman ruled until 1360. If he had reigned for twenty-four years and his predecessor respectively held the throne for four years, then Musa must have died in 1332. Of course, as with most elements of the Mali Empire's history, nothing is known for sure. Regardless of the exact timeline, historians are fairly certain that Suleyman ruled for twenty-four years, which either means that Mansa Musa died in 1332 or that he abdicated the throne, passing it to his son before he died. It is possible that Musa might not have been in a fit state to rule.

Overall, despite garnering a negative reputation, Mansa Suleyman was, subjectively, a rather good leader. In the twenty-four years he spent ruling over the Mali Empire, its economy flourished and recovered from the elaborate spending of his predecessor. Although tensions were growing, Suleyman managed to keep the kingdom mostly under control, and other than the loss of the Dyolof province, the Mali Empire's territory remained pretty much unscathed, despite the number of rebellions and land wars.

On top of all of the issues, Suleyman also had to deal with the Black Death, which was a devastating pandemic of bubonic plague that affected most of the world in the 14th century. It hit Africa hard. The Black Death is recorded as the deadliest pandemic to have ever occurred. It is unknown exactly how many people died in Africa, but the African continent as a whole was not hit as hard as Europe. It devasted North Africa, though, and it also reached Mali, likely due to the trade routes. The plague wiped out a good chunk of the population. While much of Europe suffered terrible financial losses on top of massive fatality rates, the Mali Empire managed to keep its economy stable during the pandemic. The plague would certainly explain Suleyman's financial strictness. Although historians could certainly debate the following statement, it is very likely that Mansa Suleyman endured the most difficult period as ruler of the Mali Empire. Though he is not mentioned nearly as often as Sundiata or Musa, he was by far one of the Mali Empire's most impressive mansas.

All of that being said, while Mansa Suleyman would manage to hold the Mali Empire together during his reign, his successor would inherit, other than the economy, an entirely unstable empire. With increasing rebellions, growing dissatisfaction, and serious cracks within the royal family, the empire's glory days were over.

Chapter 6 – The Continuation of the Faga Laye Lineage and the Downfall of the Mali Empire (1360–1389)

Mansa Kassa (or Mansa Camba)

In 1360, Mansa Suleyman died of unknown causes and was succeeded by his son, who was known as Kassa or Camba. Almost nothing is known about Mansa Kassa's life or his reign. However, when he inherited the throne from his father, it would seem he inherited not only all of his difficulties but also all of his enemies as well. Kassa would only hold the throne for nine months before being overthrown by one of Mansa Maghan's sons (Mansa Musa's grandson), known as Mari Djata II or Djatal.

Mansa Mari Djata II

Mansa Mari Djata II, also known as Djatal and by his original name of Konkodougou Kamissa, would claim the throne for himself in 1360 after killing Mansa Kassa. Though the murder of his predecessor may seem sudden or villainous, it was many years coming. Some even believed that Mansa Mari Djata II was actually in the right for his actions. Even before Mansa Suleyman's wife Qasa conspired against her husband and demanded that Djata take the throne, he was plotting his future kill. It has to be remembered that much of the royal family believed that Mansa Suleyman actually disposed of Mansa Maghan, Mansa Musa's son, in order to claim the throne for himself. Seeing that Mari Djata II was the son of Mansa Maghan, many considered the killing of Suleyman's son, Kassa, to be a fair form of retribution.

According to reports, it is believed by historians that after being contacted by Qasa's slave, Mari Djata fled the Mali Empire, plotting his accession to the throne. After spending years in a foreign country and when he felt the time was right, Mari Djata II returned to the Mali Empire and disposed of Mansa Kassa, only nine months after he took over for his father. Mari Djata II was likely aided in his plot, as the royal family and the empire's administration were completely divided and feuding at this time.

Although Mansa Mari Djata II may have been supported by a portion of both the administration and population, he is considered to be one of the worst mansas in the history of the Mali Empire. Mansa Mari Djata was said to be an extremely oppressive, tyrannical, and downright cruel ruler. Though Suleyman was described as strict, his rigidness was mostly for the betterment of the kingdom. Mansa Djata II, on the other hand, was said to be a selfish ruler who did little to improve the lives of the people.

This, of course, was not a good time for a self-interested mansa to be ruling, as the empire was already discontent with the monarchy. Mansa Mari Djata II spent money wastefully, and his spending only further aggravated the population and royal family. Unlike Mansa Musa, who was said to live a very lavish lifestyle, Mansa Djata II did not invest any money back into the empire's economy, education, culture, or society. Rather than searching for ways to earn more money from his resources, Mansa Djata II taxed his people at an insanely unmanageable level, contributing further to the population's dissatisfaction. Perhaps the only positive thing that Mansa Mari Djata II managed to do during his reign was to maintain positive foreign relations, specifically with Morocco. Apparently, he was even reported to have sent a giraffe to Morocco's king at the time, Hassan of the Maghreb, in order to gain favor.

Assuming that Mansa Suleyman was, in fact, Musa's brother and not his son, Mansa Mari Djata II restored Musa's immediate lineage in the dynasty. However, that being said, he did not live up to his grandfather's reputation. Though the Mali Empire was crumbling under Mansa Suleyman, it was Mansa Djata II who is credited with putting the final nails in the coffin.

In the words of Ibn Khaldun, an Arab of Berber descent who was a famous historian and author and who is still renowned for his works on philosophy and sociology, "Mari Djata, the son of Mansa Maghan, the son of Mansa Musa, reigned for fourteen years. He was a bad ruler who oppressed the people, depleted the treasury and nearly pulled down the structure of the government. Finally he was attacked by sleeping sickness and died within two years of its onset." Mansa Djata II would pass away in 1374. He served for fourteen years, and in that time, Mansa Mari Djata II brought the empire to its end. However, historians debate whether it would have collapsed at this point anyway due to the tensions and dissatisfaction in the administration, the royal family, and the population. Either way, Mansa Djata certainly did not help to prevent the collapse in any way.

Between 1372 and 1374, while Mansa Djata II was sick, the Mali Empire was controlled by his ministers, who did little during their stint in power. They had no real positive or negative effect, and the kingdom continued barreling toward its end.

Mansa Musa II

Mansa Mari Djata II was succeeded by his son, Mansa Musa II, named after his great-grandfather, the illustrious Mansa Musa. Mansa Musa II reigned more in the style of his namesake rather than his father, as he attempted to restore the Mali Empire to its former glory. In the words of Ibn Khaldun, "After him [Mansa Djata II], they gave the throne to his son Musa. He followed the path of justice and departed from the way of his father."

As Mansa Suleyman found out years before, restoring and keeping control of an empire as large as the Mali Empire in the 14th century was not easy and could not be done alone. According to historian Ibn Khaldun, who provided modern historians with much of their knowledge of the Mali Empire at this time, "His [Mansa Musa II] chief minister Mari Djata assumed the reins of the government and kept Musa, the Sultan, secluded. Mari Djata mobilized armies and subdued the countries that laid to the east of their lands." In other words, Mansa Musa II had good intentions, but he actually did little himself. In fact, most of the power and decisions were in the hands of his chief minister. Mansa Musa II's chief minister was known as Mari Djata, and he was the real ruler of the Mali Empire during this time. Though Mansa Musa II acted as a figurehead and likely had the power to veto laws and policies, he had little involvement in any decisions during his fourteen years on the throne.

While some historians would describe Mansa Musa II as weak, it was for the best that the empire was in the hands of Mari Djata, as he is likely the only reason the empire did not collapse entirely. Mari Djata seemed to have an almost natural intuition when it came to leading, and as mentioned by Ibn Khaldun, he mobilized armies and subdued nearby regions, which were likely in revolt.

The two main revolts that broke out during Mansa Musa II's reign were that of the Songhai, who remained in Gao, and that of the Tuareg population in Takedda and Timbuktu. Although Mansa Musa I had conquered the Gao region for the Mali Empire and built up its structures around 1325, the war for the land had never truly been over for its original owners. While much of the world had loved and admired the original Mansa Musa, the Songhai people, who had reigned over the Gao region for centuries before he came along, did not share the same love. They did not cheer as the tenth mansa of the Mali Empire rode into their city, ridiculed their king, and took his two sons as prisoners. Though Mansa Musa built Mali-style buildings in Gao, the Songhai population remained, and most of them not only never got over the conquering of their land but also never considered themselves to be a part of the Mali Empire. While they would stage various rebellions over the course of the 14th century, it would not be until the empire's end that the Songhai population would be able to compete with the Mali Empire's competent military.

During the late 14th century, the Mali Empire's administration was fighting many internal battles, and while the empire's military was large, it was spread very thin trying to defend the massive kingdom. Although the exact dates are unknown, historians believe that it was during Mansa Musa II's reign that the Mali Empire officially lost the Gao region to the Songhai people, despite intense fighting for the territory. It is possible that the Mali Empire had actually lost part of the Gao region beforehand, as some historians believe that it actually occurred in the 1360s under Mansa Mari Djata II's reign. Regardless of the debate, the entire region was officially brought back under the Songhai people's control during Mansa Musa II's reign. This victory for the Songhai people marked a new beginning for the Songhai state, which would eventually transform into an empire and annex the Mali Empire. Although Mari Djata (Musa II's advisor) would continue to send troops to campaign in Gao to try and win the territory back for the Mali Empire, his attempts were continuously thwarted by the Songhai people.

The other population that Mari Djata attempted to fend off was Tuaregs, who had inhabited Mali long before the mansas ruled. Although you can find mentions of the Tuareg people in historical accounts of life in the 14th century, very few historians actually met the Tuareg people, which was the case for historian Ibn Khaldun. While citizens, settlers, merchants, and students may have seen the veiled Tuaregs walking around the Mali Empire, specifically in the city that they created, Timbuktu, they remained a somewhat mysterious population that kept to themselves. That being said, despite being more secular than other populations, the Tuaregs shared a common dislike for their territory's monarchy and administration.

Much like the Songhai people, over the course of the 14th century, the Tuaregs were constantly waging wars, rebellions, and revolts, attempting to reclaim their land. However, unlike the Songhai people, the Tuaregs would not successfully reconquer their land. Instead, the Mali Empire's military, as instructed by Mari Djata, would continue to put down the many Tuareg rebellions.

Mari Djata, or technically Mansa Musa II, would rule the Mali Empire until 1387, which was when the latter of the two died. Although the two of them had inherited a collapsing empire from Mansa Djata II, they managed to prolong its life for a little while longer. While Mari Djata was an excellent leader, he was not a miracle worker. Despite the fact that the Mali Empire managed to remain somewhat stable for fourteen years during the reign of the figurehead Mansa Musa II, it was still heading toward its dissolution.

During the reign of Mansa Musa II, the Mali Empire was technically in a civil war, as the administration attempted to fight the people who were dissatisfied with the monarchy. While the empire did not lose too much land during the rebellions, it was more like a bandage on a burgeoning floodgate. Apart from the internal issues that the Mali Empire was facing, the continent of Africa was suffering as well. Though Mansa Musa II and Mari Djata had managed to fix the Mali Empire's economy, it was nowhere near its once former glory, and in the later years of the 14th century, trade cities throughout most of Africa were taking a hit. Historians and economists believe the reason for Africa's sudden economic downfall was the mass construction of trade centers, which essentially meant trade was no longer just occurring in a few cities. With people spending money among many trade centers in many empires, it meant less money concentrated in a few centers.

In modern financial terms, during Mansa Musa I's reign, the Mali Empire was in a bull market; the economy was continuing to improve, and that rise did not seem to be going anywhere. However, after the death of Mansa Musa I, who was one of the Mali Empire's most money-savvy kings, his successors either squandered away money or struggled to adapt to the changing markets. The Mali Empire's finances were not improved by the constant wars of the late 14th century. The Mali Empire lost territory, specifically that of Gao, which had become a large source of commercial activity. Furthermore, with the growing dissatisfaction of the population, much of the Mali Empire was being raided, both by external and internal populations. In Timbuktu, the Tuareg population changed their rebellion style; instead of revolting violently, they simply began appropriating tax money rather than sending it to Mansa Musa II or his administration.

Really, it was the intelligent leaders such as Mari Djata and Suleyman who were holding the empire together at this point, but there was no way subsequent kings could continue staying that course. It was as if every administration change went one step forward and two steps back. The issues within the empire were gradually growing too large for just one leader to control, and with the monarchical system of ancient Africa still in place, the Mali Empire was at the end of its lifespan.

Mansa Maghan II

After the death of Mansa Musa II in 1387, he was succeeded by his brother Mansa Maghan II, who was named after his grandfather. Very little is known of Mansa Maghan II's reign, but it is believed that, like his brother, Maghan II simply acted as a figurehead, with the actual administration being led by the officers of the court. Unlike Mari Djata, Mansa Maghan II's officers did very little, and it is likely that the empire's issues only continued to worsen since they made little effort to change anything. Finally, after two years, the mansa of the Mali Empire was deposed by his successor (it is unknown if he was simply removed from the throne, killed, or imprisoned). This put an end to the Faga Laye lineage, which had begun with the great Mansa Musa in 1312.

Within the seventy-seven years of the Faga Laye lineage, the state of the Mali Empire had essentially transformed into the most powerful and wealthy empire of Africa until finally crumbling into a shell of its former glory. If the once-great Mali Empire had a chance of surviving after Mansa Musa II's and Mari Djata's impressive reigns, it was certainly not by deposing the monarch. This violent accession to the throne would only aid in worsening the cracks in the administration and angering the rest of the population who still respected the royal family.

Chapter 7 – The Final Mansas of the Mali Empire and Its Collapse (1389–the Beginning of the 17th century)

Mansa Sandaki

After the death of Musa II, the throne passed to his brother, Maghan II. Although he, like his brother, simply acted as a figurehead during his reign, the administration was no longer in the hands of Mari Djata but instead shared between numerous officers of the court.

After only two years on the throne, Mansa Maghan II was captured and imprisoned. It is believed he was murdered by Mansa Sandaki, a usurper who would take the throne for himself. It is not known for sure who Mansa Sandaki was exactly or why and how he claimed the throne. Some historians believe Mansa Sandaki was Mari Djata himself, reclaiming the administration after not being allowed to continue running the Mali Empire following the death of Mansa Musa II. The more common belief is that Mansa Sandaki was a relative of Mari Djata.

To make matters even more confusing, Mari Djata is the name used to refer to Mansa Sundiata, Mansa Djata II, and Mansa Sandaki, as well as Mansa Musa II's chief minister. In reports done by historians and writers of the time, all four of the previously mentioned men are referred to as Mari Djata, though writers often cycled through their various names. This shared namesake leads historians to believe that Mansa Sandaki was, in fact, a relative of Mansa Sundiata himself. However, all of that being said, whether Sandaki was actually a descendent of Sundiata or Mari Djata is not known for sure, but being a relative of either of the aforementioned leaders may explain Sandaki's decision to claim the throne for himself.

Although Sandaki's exact relations are not known, it makes sense that he claimed the throne, as he more than likely felt he was deserving of it due to his lineage. This would have likely been supported by other members of the royal family and administration, making his accession far easier. To make matters even more confusing (yet again), some historians believe that Mansa Sandaki actually married Mansa Djata II's widowed wife (Musa II's mother.) This would have not only brought some more legitimacy to Sandaki's name but also muddied up his lineage, making it difficult to know for sure if he was a relative of the former mansas due to his blood or his marriage.

All of Mansa Sandaki's confusing lineage has led to a lot of debates as to whether Sandaki was another member of the Keita dynasty or not. This is important because if Mansa Sandaki was, in fact, a member of the Keita dynasty, it would mean that the Keita dynasty ruled uninterrupted during the entire existence of the Mali Empire. If Sandaki was not a member of the Keita dynasty, it would mean he brought about the end of the original dynasty, making his accession to the throne even more scandalous and demonstrative of the cracks in the empire at this time.

Whether Mansa Sandaki is related to other mansas remains unknown, but what is known is that his and his successors' obscure origins are a powerful example of the Mali Empire's unsteady administration. Despite all of the drama that Sandaki caused to claim the throne for himself, he did very little with his time as mansa. After less than one year as ruler, maybe only a few months, Mansa Sandaki was killed and replaced by Maghan III.

Mansa Maghan III

Similar to his predecessor, Maghan III's exact relation to the royal lineage is not known for certain, but many historians believe him to be a relative of Mansa Gao. While it is believed that Maghan III's accession may have brought the Keita lineage back onto the throne, it is not actually known for sure if Maghan III was even a relative of any member of the Keita dynasty, let alone Mansa Gao.

Maghan III was crowned as mansa in 1390, and during his time in charge, he managed to achieve more than some of his predecessors. But, of course, this is to be expected, as he ruled longer than either of the two mansas before him. Despite having killed his predecessor, the most pressing issue was not his unconventional (though it was becoming conventional at this time) rise to mansa but rather keeping the Mali Empire intact. There were likely many internal and external threats to the Mali Empire due to the growing tensions within the empire and with neighboring regions.

Few of the conflicts the Mali Empire faced at the end of the 14th century are known to historians. Writers of the time spoke of the pressing issue of the Mossi Emperor Bonga of Yatenga's raids of the Mali Empire. While there were raids throughout much of the empire at this time, the Mossi raids in Mali and Macina (an important trading post located in modern-day south-central Mali) were some of the worst, as Emperor Bonga of Yatenga was close to conquering part of the empire's territory for his own empire.

During his reign, Mansa Maghan III would manage to hold off Emperor Bonga of Yatenga's raids and attempts to capture land, and when Maghan III died in 1400, much, if not all, of the empire remained intact.

The Mossi Empire

Since the Mossi Empire played a vital role in the Mali Empire's history, a short history of the empire has been included here. The Mossi Empire was made up of various small kingdoms that were located around the Volta River in modern-day Ghana and Burkina Faso. Similar to the other empires, the Mossi Empire started off small, with minor kingdoms gradually joining with other kingdoms. In the 13th century, after the Mossi Empire had grown too large to continue to be run with several independent kingdoms, power was centralized, which led to some internal conflict. Many revolutions were waged against Komdimie, who was Mossi's emperor in the late 1100s to the early 1200s. One of the most notable of these revolutions was executed by the Mossi Kingdom of Yatenga. Warring within the Mossi Empire only helped to strengthen its military and grow the government. In the end, the Kingdom of Yatenga won independence and more land, and all of the Mossi kingdoms were given more autonomy from the emperor. By the end of the 14th century, every kingdom within the Mossi Empire had its own strong military, which focused on soldiers and cavalries traveling light in order to cover large distances quicker than other armies.

Throughout the 14th century, the Mossi Empire continued to fight off threats from nearby kingdoms, and by the beginning of the 15th century, they were strong enough to begin being seen as a threat themselves. The Mossi and the Songhai Empires had been battling for nearly half a century, and eventually, Mossi began harassing the Mali Empire as well. Despite constantly warring with the Songhai Empire, the Mossi attacks and raids in the Mali Empire would end up aiding the Songhai Empire in defeating Mali. At the end of the

15th century, the Songhai Empire would defeat the Mossi Empire, yet the small kingdoms resisted change. When the Songhai Empire fell a century later, the Mossi Empire would rebuild and remain an entity until the European invasion centuries later.

Mansa Musa III

After Mansa Maghan III's death, Musa III took the throne. Despite the fact that the Mali Empire had been slowly collapsing throughout the reign of the past few mansas, another Musa would somehow return some of its former glory. Similar to his predecessors before him, little is known about Mansa Musa III's exact heritage. It is not known, for instance, whether he was entitled to the throne or not, and while he is often referred to as a Keita, it is not known for sure if he was related to the once-powerful dynasty.

Through interpreting orally transmitted histories, it is believed that before Musa III was crowned as mansa, his brother led the Mali Empire's military into a region south of Niani known as Dioma. Mansa III and his younger brother proceeded to drive out the previous population of Dioma, who were known as the Fula (Peuhl) Wassoulounké. They conquered Dioma for the Mali Empire. It is assumed this was achieved at the tail end of Mansa Maghan III's reign, so it is possible that Musa III was crowned as the new mansa after Maghan III died for his incredible achievement and displays of strength, bravery, and leadership potential. It is also possible that Mansa Musa III was not officially crowned until a few years after the death of Mansa Maghan III. If that was the case, the empire was likely run by officers of the court while they awaited a mansa who could keep the empire alive. The officers of the court were likely impressed by Musa III's acquisition of Dioma and decided he would be the best candidate for the throne.

While Mansa Musa III managed to return the Mali Empire to some of its former grandeur by conquering territory, which had not been done in decades, once he was crowned as mansa, he was not as successful in saving the empire. Although Mansa Maghan III had managed to fight off the Mossi raids led by Bonga of Yatenga, there were just too many conflicts at once to protect the gradually collapsing empire by the time Musa III took the throne.

Whether it was before or during his reign, Mansa Musa III certainly took part in the intensive war against the Fula people, whom Mansa Suleyman had actually battled many decades prior. Meanwhile, the Mali Empire was battling for some of its greatest trade cities. Timbuktu had been divided for years now between the Tuareg population, which it once belonged to, and the Mali Empire's administration, which still currently controlled and profited from the city. Although the exact dates of the battles are unknown, it is likely that the Tuareg population continued revolting and attempting to claim Timbuktu and their previous land throughout the reigns of many mansas. At the start of Mansa Musa III's reign in 1400, he was forced to send mass numbers of troops to Timbuktu in order to battle the Tuareg people.

However, the Mali Empire's military was not what it once was. After losing faith in the royal family and administration, as well as the Mali Empire's loss of territory, the empire's army had weakened. Though there was likely a form of conscription forcing able men to join the forces, they were no longer fighting to honor their kingdom but out of requirement. This meant that the empire's army was not only shorthanded in Timbuktu, as the military was spread pretty thin over the warring Mali Empire, but also not as passionate, well trained, or invested in the campaigns against the Tuaregs as previous generations of the army had been.

The Tuareg people, on the other hand, were fighting with everything they had. Although the exact date of when Timbuktu was acquired by the Mali Empire is unknown, the Tuaregs had likely been under the control of the Mali Empire for nearly a century at this point. Tales of how the Tuaregs had once controlled Timbuktu and other territories in the Mali Empire were told throughout the generations of Tuaregs, thus continuing the rivalry between the two groups. Finally, in 1430, after decades of battle, the Tuareg people managed to defeat the endless men sent by the Mali Empire and succeeded in winning back Timbuktu.

However, Timbuktu was only the start. After their massive win, the Tuaregs were determined to gain back more of the territory that had been stolen from them by the Mali Empire's mansas, and so, the battles over territory continued throughout the following years. By 1433, the Tuaregs had also managed to win back Oualata (Walata), which had been one of the largest stops on the trans-Saharan trade routes before Mansa Musa I had commissioned architects and designers to build up Timbuktu.

The land gained by the Tuareg people, specifically Timbuktu, was a massive loss to the Mali Empire. However, there was little that Mansa Musa III could do. The Tuaregs' success in gaining their territories back had been decades in the making, and throughout the many rebellions, raids, and revolts conducted by the Tuaregs in Timbuktu over the years, the Tuaregs had managed to weaken enforcement in the city and slowly regain control. By Mansa Musa III's reign, the Tuaregs were no longer paying taxes to the administration, and they were no longer following instructions. In other words, they were essentially running the city. While there were most likely many other battles during the reign of Mansa Musa III, the only one known to modern historians is that with the Tuaregs.

Since the exact date of Mansa Musa III's crowning is unknown, it is estimated he ruled the Mali Empire for approximately sixty years. Although his long reign would have brought some stability back to the empire, his reign was seen as far from stable since he faced constant threats from all over the empire and throughout his entire reign. Overall, despite Mansa Musa III's early promise as a leader, his reign is regarded overall as a loss for the empire, although that has more to do with his timing than his actual leadership skills, as he had inherited a collapsing kingdom.

Mansa Uli II

Although Timbuktu was no longer in the hands of the Mali Empire, it is important to continue learning about the Mali Empire's history to fully grasp the history of Timbuktu. This is because the empire that would eventually conquer the remains of the once-great Mali Empire would eventually come to conquer Timbuktu.

After the death of Mansa Musa III, the throne was passed to his brother Gbèré, who had also taken part in leading the conquest of Dioma. Crowned as Mansa Uli II, Gbèré began his reign in 1460. On top of inheriting all of the issues that his brother faced as mansa, Uli II had to deal with the threat of European invasion, as well as a growing Songhai state (it would become an empire in 1464).

Around a decade before Mansa Uli II inherited the throne, Portugal had begun sending troops to the coasts of Africa with the intention of gaining and raiding territories. Since some of the northwestern coasts of Africa were under the control of Mali at this time, Portugal's expeditions caused great conflict for the already struggling Mali Empire. Although Portuguese explorers would eventually form relations with civilians and the administration in the Mali Empire, these positive foreign relations would come too late, as Portugal's effects had already proven to be disastrous for the suffering empire. Despite the interference of the Portuguese, the Mali Empire managed to maintain its supremacy in the west, along the coast of Africa.

Unfortunately, the same could not be said of the rest of the Mali Empire. The conflicts with Portugal had weakened the Mali Empire's army, and they accidentally served as a distraction for the Songhai Empire, which was waging wars for territory in the north and northeast of the Mali Empire. First, the Songhai Empire conquered Mema in 1465, which was a part of Mansa Sundiata's original acquisitions from the Ghana Empire when he formed his empire. Over the following years, the Songhai Empire continued to wage wars for various territories within and around the Mali Empire. Within three years of acquiring Mema, the Songhai Empire, which at this time was led by Sonni Ali Ber, actually managed to seize Timbuktu from the Tuaregs. Not much is known of what the Tuaregs did in Timbuktu after they initially seized it from the Mali Empire. However, they were undoubtedly not pleased by the Songhai Empire's acquisition of their territory, especially so soon after they got it back.

The Final Mansas of the Mali Empire
Mansa Mahmud II

The exact dates of Mansa Mahmud II's reign are unknown for sure, as are his origins; however, he is believed to have taken the throne sometime around the late 1470s or early 1480s. While Mansa Mahmud II was not the first mansa to inherit problems surrounding the empire's collapse, his reign was marked by more losses and difficulties than most of his successors. Many of the issues that his predecessors faced either continued into Mansa Mahmud II's reign or worsened.

This is especially true of the Mossi raids in the Mali Empire. Nasséré, the emperor of Yatenga, was just as, if not more intense than his predecessor. This time, the Mossi raids were successful, and Nasséré managed to conquer the province of BaGhana (Wagadou) in 1477 for Yatenga. (BaGhana and Wagadou are names that were used at the time for a territory that had been occupied by the Ghana Empire in modern-day southeastern Mauritania and western Mali.)

That would not be the only loss of territory during Mansa Mahmud II's reign. In the early 1480s, the Fula began raiding the Takrur provinces. In 1481, the Mali Empire would officially lose Jalo (Fouta Djallon; located in modern-day Guinea), and only two years later, the Songhai people conquered the salt mines of Taghaza (located in Mali's northern desert region), which had been profitable during previous mansas' reigns.

Meanwhile, communications between the Mali Empire and Portugal continued, as the latter continued to send explorers to the coast of Africa. Although the Mali Empire was crumbling, they still had products to trade, and over the course of Mansa Mahmud II's reign, trade with Portugal intensified. When the Fula raids started getting serious for the Mali Empire, they actually sent a request for aid from Portugal, which Portugal declined, likely because it was not beneficial enough to the Portuguese to get involved. It is uncertain exactly when Mansa Mahmud II passed the throne to his successor, but it is believed that he did not reign into the 16th century.

Mansa Mahmud III

Mansa Mahmud III inherited the Mali Empire. There were many territories on the verge of being lost, and wars broke out all over the kingdom. During his reign, the Mali Empire reached out again to Portugal for aid in fighting the various raids. However, it was of no use, as the Mali Empire was reaching its end. On top of the other issues Mansa Mahmud III inherited when he took the throne, a massive Mali Empire military region known as Kaabu became independent in 1537. The men from Kaabu took not only the Kaabu region itself but also the nearby territories of Cassa and Bati. In 1545, Mansa Mahmud III was forced to flee from Niani, the capital city of the Mali Empire. After intensive battles, Niani was sacked and conquered by the Songhai Empire. This was on top of all the raids by the Yatenga and Fula tribes. In other words, the Mali Empire only held a small percentage of the landmass and power it once ruled over.

Mansa Mahmud IV

Mahmud IV would be the last mansa of the Mali Empire, although his actual reign had little impact on what was about to happen. After all, Mahmud IV inherited a crumbling empire. Although the Mali Empire had many rivals at this time, its main threat was that the growing Songhai Empire, which had once been a part of the Mali Empire (albeit not as an empire but as a state). While the Mali Empire was facing many threats by the mid-16th century, you had to wonder what would have become of the Mali Empire had Mansa Musa not acquired Gao and ridiculed the leader of the Songhai state almost two centuries before.

Mansa Mahmud IV attempted to save the Mali Empire the best he could by launching attacks into previously acquired regions, such as Djenné, and allying with smaller kingdoms in order to fight the powerful Songhai and Fula kingdoms. Moroccan soldiers from Timbuktu, which had been wrested from the Songhai Empire and placed under Morocco's control by this time, were also waging firearm attacks on not only the Mali Empire but also the Songhai Empire. The Mali Empire stood strong against the Moroccan threats, but Mansa Mahmud IV and his people were finally forced to flee to the Kangaba region, which still remained a part of the Mali Empire.

Although the Mali Empire held onto a small portion of its original territory, which was split between Mansa Mahmud IV's sons after his death, there would be no more mansas, putting an official end to the once-great Mali Empire. Each of Mahmud IV's sons would continue to reign over their smaller territories, which each could be considered a smaller kingdom. After wars and land transfers, these small kingdoms would eventually transform into the modern-day country of Mali.

Chapter 8 – The Songhai Empire (1464–1591)

The Early Years of the Songhai Empire

As mentioned previously, the Songhai people had inhabited the territory of what would become the Songhai Empire even before the establishment of the Mali Empire. In a similar timeframe to the creation of the Mali Empire, in around the 11th century or so, it is believed that the Songhai people officially named the city of Gao as their capital city and created the Songhai Kingdom, which at that time revolved around the nearby Niger River for transport and food, as well as Islamic religious and cultural beliefs. By the time of Mansa Musa I's rule, the Songhai state, specifically its original Gao region, had become successful and financially stable. It was well established, and best of all, it was a large hub for trade and Muslim scholars, all of which attracted the Mali Empire to it.

Just to quickly recap, sometime around 1325, the Mali Empire was said to have acquired Gao and swallowed the Songhai Kingdom. To make Mali's conquering known to all in the region, Mansa Musa himself rode into Gao and forced the leader of the Songhai people to submit completely. Musa then proceeded to take the Songhai king's sons as prisoners. The Mali Empire continued to build upon Gao's already established resources, transforming it into a more successful city, while the Songhai people who remained in the territory plotted ways to avenge their loss and regain their territory. The Songhai population would launch small revolts and rebellions for decades after losing their territory to the Mali Empire. Finally, between the 1360s and 1370s, they managed to win back Gao and restart their kingdom, which would eventually become an empire. Over the course of the decline of the Mali Empire, the Songhai Empire acquired more of Mali's territories and resources.

Sonni Ali

Sonni Ali, also known as Sonni (or Sunni) Ali Ber, which translates to Ali the Great, was the first leader of the Songhai Empire. Estimated to have reigned between 1464 and 1492, Sonni Ali is somewhat of a controversial leader. Although he was incredibly intelligent and powerful and is credited with elevating the Songhai Empire's strength and power, he was also considered to be cruel, intolerant, and destructive. While Sonni Ali may have invaded and acquired the great city of Timbuktu from the Tuareg people, he also destroyed the city in the process, not only by knocking down its incredible structures in war but also by enforcing strict laws against education, specifically Tuareg scholars. A similar destructive course of action took place in the conquest of Djenné, which took Sonni Ali seven years of warring to acquire. In the process, he almost starved the entire population of Djenné to death. Nonetheless, he achieved great things for the Songhai Empire, and like many leaders of his time, he cared very little for the regions or people he ruined in the process.

In addition to acquiring the great cities of Timbuktu and Djenné, the Songhai Empire under Sonni Ali went on to conquer much of the remaining Mali Empire. Although many territories were destroyed in the process of acquiring them, Sonni Ali and his successors worked to rebuild the once great cities they conquered. Soon enough, even Timbuktu was restored to resemble much of its former self. Sonni Ali, like his predecessors and successors, was a devout Muslim; therefore, it would make sense that he would rebuild Timbuktu and the other Mali Empire cities they acquired as a place for Islamic learning. Under Sonni Ali, the Songhai Empire's original territory of Gao also developed and grew.

Sonni Ali's devotion to his faith only intensified as he embarked on a pilgrimage to Mecca; however, for Ali, the hajj was not just about religion. Along the way to Saudi Arabia, Sonni Ali waged various wars, which allowed him to expand the borders of the Songhai Empire even farther. Although he did not force his religion on his population, much of his policies and architectural projects were inspired by Islam. By the end of his reign, the Songhai Empire had grown to include over 1,400,000 square kilometers and was significantly larger than what remained of the Mali Empire. It also included much of modern-day western Sudan.

Askia the Great

Sonni Ali was followed by his son, who was deposed and replaced by Askia the Great (Muhammad). The name implies it already, but Askia is considered to be another formidable leader of the Songhai Empire. Although Sonni Ali had already grown the Songhai Empire until it overwhelmed and eventually swallowed what was left of the Mali Empire, Askia the Great would gain many more territories for the kingdom, transforming the Songhai Empire into the largest empire in the history of West Africa. It is even believed to be larger than the Mali Empire once was. The Songhai Empire was soon a large enough territory to trade with massive European and Asian kingdoms as an equal.

Similar to the leaders before him, Askia the Great was a devout Muslim, and although he did not force his population to convert, he invested heavily in Islamic schools, mosques, and artists. His love of Islamic studies attracted scholars, poets, and artists from all over the world, and soon, the Songhai Empire became the home to many iconic pieces of art and new developing studies, such as astronomy. On top of investing heavily in Islamic studies, Askia invested time and funds into his government, cities, economy, and agriculture.

As is necessary with all growing empires, by the time of Askia the Great's reign, the Songhai Empire was in need of a new administration organization, as it had outgrown its previous one. Similar to the Mali Empire, the Songhai Empire separated its territories into smaller regions, which were each governed by individual governors. However, unlike the Mali Empire, the Songhai kept the power more centralized, as all of the region's administrators were royal appointees who communicated and received orders directly from Askia the Great himself.

Askia the Great split the Songhai Empire into five separate provinces, each with its own tax collection service, Islamic courts, administration, and military. The tax collection services and military worked together to ensure that all farmers paid taxes, which were known as tribute, to Askia the Great. Due to the prevalence of farming, tax collection on farms and their products, as well as trade, was one of the primary streams of income for the Songhai Empire. Some of the main products grown and traded in the Songhai Empire during Askia the Great's reign were kola nuts, gold, slaves, salt, cowries, horses, and cloth.

Gradually, as Askia the Great brought in more territories, the empire acquired the aforementioned industries and other products and resources, which helped enlarge the Songhai Empire's economy. Since agriculture was the main source of income for the empire, Askia the Great had canals built throughout the main farming lands, which, in turn, helped grow trade and the economy further. A lesser-known but thoroughly interesting change that Askia the Great introduced was that of proper weights and measurements of products, which, until that point, was usually estimated and thus inaccurate.

However, despite all of Askia's great accomplishments as king, he would face an issue that had plagued the leaders of the Mali Empire and eventually helped lead to its downfall: family drama. It is estimated that Askia the Great remained on the throne between 1493 and 1528, and by the end of his thirty-five-year reign, he started to lose respect, power, and control, perhaps due to his old age. In 1528, Askia the Great would be overthrown by his sons, and by 1531, his son Askia Musa claimed the throne for himself.

The instability at the top led to instability throughout the Songhai Empire, and as surrounding regions attempted to raid territories and resources from the weakened Songhai, the kings had little understanding of how to defend the massive kingdom. Gradually, the Songhai Empire declined and lost power. This actually happened around the same time the Mali Empire collapsed. In 1591, the Moroccans, equipped with firearms, would officially conquer the Songhai Empire. Although there are many reasons for the fall of the Songhai Empire, most historians credit the eventual collapse to not only the family drama, which distracted the centralized administration, but also to the Songhai Empire's failure to modernize their army. As they remained stuck in their old ways, other regions around them acquired firearms and other advanced weapons.

Timbuktu during the Songhai Empire

Just as it had been at the height of the Mali Empire's reign, the Songhai kings transformed the city of Timbuktu into a glorious, diverse hub for trade, education, religion, and culture. By the time the Songhai Empire started building up Timbuktu, global travel and trade had grown exponentially. This means that at its peak, the Songhai Empire's Timbuktu was home to not only Arab and African born merchants and settlers but also immigrants and merchants from all sorts of backgrounds and countries, including a large population of both Italian and Jewish merchants. Although there were trade cities throughout the entirety of the Songhai

Empire, including the great city of Gao, Timbuktu had once again become a favorite stop for travelers. And with its advanced libraries, schools, and mosques, it became home, once again, to some of the 16th century's greatest scholars and artists.

Throughout the Songhai Empire, there was a clan system, which somewhat resembles the caste system of India. This was especially true in massive trade cities such as Timbuktu. One's occupation and lifestyle depended entirely on one's birth clan. At the bottom, there were slaves and war captives, who were mostly forced to farm. Above them, there were farmers making small salaries and then non-farmer immigrants who worked various unwanted jobs in the kingdom. Then there were the common fishermen, carpenters, metal-workers, and others. Both the immigrant non-farmers and the common workers could have some form of upward mobility into higher position jobs, depending on their connections. Finally, at the top of the food chain, there were noblemen, freemen, and traders, who usually were either related to Songhai's elite families or were very wealthy.

As mentioned above, much of Askia the Great's policies were based on Islamic principles, as was the case for criminal justice in not only Timbuktu but also all of the Songhai Empire. Although criminal justice was used more for cases involving lower-class citizens than the elites, it was the upper-class citizens who actually followed Islamic practices and had an understanding of Islamic principles. Most of the lower-class citizens kept following the traditional religions.

Chapter 9 – The Downfall of the Songhai Empire, the Moroccan Occupation, and the French Invasion (1591–1900)

The Collapse of the Songhai Empire

As mentioned above, the Songhai Empire would collapse because of the Moroccan army. This was mostly due to the drama within the administration and the enemy's stronger and more advanced weapons. However, these were not the only reasons for the Songhai Empire's downfall. The armed Moroccans started by conquering the Songhai Empire's income sources, such as the trade cities of Gao and Timbuktu and the salt mines at Taghaza. Before long, Morocco occupied the trans-Saharan trade routes, blocking the path of any Songhai merchant and preventing the empire from earning money from trade.

Meanwhile, non-Songhai people within and surrounding the empire began to form independent states; among these were the Hausa, Bornu, and Tuareg people. This only served to further decrease trade and income. The countries that were left to trade with no longer had as large of a demand for the products of the Songhai Empire. This was especially true in regards to gold, which was not as beloved by the 17th century. As trade continued to expand globally, countries that had once crossed the Sahara to trade with the Songhai and the Mali Empires no longer had to, as similar products could be accessed with less intensive travel.

When the majority of the Songhai Empire had finally been conquered by the Moroccans, the Songhai nobles fled to safety, mostly to the modern-day city of Songhai in Niger.

Timbuktu under Moroccan Occupation

Little is actually known about Timbuktu during the Moroccan occupation. However, it is known for sure that Timbuktu would only continue to decline after it was conquered. The city, which was officially conquered in 1591, was not used to its full potential after being conquered by Morocco. Instead, it was simply just another place to conquer. Merchants who hadn't already set up in Timbuktu had little reason to travel to the city, as there were now closer trade cities that attracted merchants from all over the world.

With no trade or merchants coming in or out and no scholars wanting to visit the city under the aggressive government, Timbuktu soon lost its grandeur and appeal. Within the next few years, the scholars and settlers who remained in Timbuktu were arrested and accused of disaffection. This was likely true, as all of the scholars and settlers who had come to Timbuktu could not have been satisfied with what the government had turned the city into. By 1593, the scholars who were arrested were either exiled to Morocco or killed if they refused to submit to the new Moroccan authority.

After defeating the Songhai Empire, the Moroccans renamed Timbuktu as its capital, replacing Gao as the capital city in the region. Although Timbuktu was occupied by the Moroccan army and was the capital city in the area, the government did not really care what happened within the city, as they were probably busy conquering other territories and managing their original population.

It was not just the scholars who were dissatisfied with the Moroccan government. Within the city of Timbuktu, there were settlers who immigrated temporarily for the mosques, schools, libraries, or trade. In addition to them, there were the Tuareg people who had originally lived in Timbuktu before it even belonged to the Mali Empire, the Bambara who make up the majority of modern-day Mali, and the Fula who had warred with the Mali Empire and conquered some of their lands. These three groups constantly rebelled and created revolts within the city. Over the course of the end of the 16th and the beginning of the 17th centuries, the city of Timbuktu was continuously passed between the control of the Bambara, Tuareg, and Fula people.

Throughout the entirety of the 17th, 18th, and 19th centuries, Timbuktu would pass between the hands of various smaller governments, none of which were able to hold onto the city. This transformed Timbuktu into more of a battleground than a livable city. As mentioned earlier, Timbuktu would never return to its former glory again, and although the Tuaregs, Bambara, Fula, and immigrant merchants and scholars in the city were dissatisfied with the Moroccan administration in Timbuktu, they did not do much more to help restore the city when they were in control. That being said, there was little reason to restore the city when it was constantly under attack and in the hands of different states.

Morocco Outside of Timbuktu

Throughout the rest of Morocco, things were much better than in Timbuktu, which, after the first few years of its conquest, was essentially abandoned by the Moroccan administration. Much like the Songhai Empire and the Mali Empire before that, the Moroccan sultan based a good portion of his political, cultural, and social systems on those of Islam. The Moroccan government focused heavily on their military, which not only had the latest weaponry and protection but was also mostly made up of slaves, meaning that the supply was essentially endless. This was especially important as Morocco continued to conquer lands and imprison those who complained or did not fully submit to its new king. Although Morocco's kings were not the first to involve themselves heavily in religion and base much of their government and society on Islamic principles, the Moroccan monarchs became known as religious leaders, which gave them more sway with the people than if they were simply just kings. This respect and power allowed them to contain rebellions, control the dissatisfied people, and calm battles between various tribes within their territory.

Though Morocco is one of the closer countries to Europe, the Moroccans remained mostly separated from the European wars, governments, and people, unlike some of the previous kingdoms before them that attempted to forge positive relations with their northern neighbors. This strategy would turn out to be at the disadvantage of the Moroccans. While Morocco kept out of European affairs, Europe planned to explore, colonize, and take advantage of territories in Africa, which at this point had been mostly unexplored by Europeans.

The French Invasion of Africa and Morocco

Although European explorers had explored much of the African coast and parts of North Africa, very few had reached Timbuktu and returned to tell the tale. Whether these explorers died along the way in the treacherous Sahara or remained in the great city is unknown. However, well into the 19th century, Timbuktu was still somewhat of a mystery to the Europeans. Although they had heard stories of gold, Mansa Musa, and the great University of Sankoré and its libraries, it would take until 1826 for any European to locate, reach, and return from Timbuktu alive, at least from what we know so far.

Although he was not the first to do so, René Caillié managed to visit and return from Timbuktu alive, and he provided Europe with much of their understanding of Timbuktu at that time. René Caillié visited Timbuktu during the period when factions were warring for power over it, not during the Moroccan reign. He would help revive the European interest in not only Timbuktu but also the regions surrounding it. While Timbuktu may not have been anywhere near what it was at its peak, its bones still showed promise, and with tales of gold, trade, and rare books, it was hard not to be interested in the mysterious city.

Two years after the journey of René Caillié, France invaded Algeria. Since Algeria and Morocco had a sort of vaguely outlined alliance at this time, Morocco actually sent over military aid to help Algeria fight off the European threat. However, after the French began protesting, Moroccan Sultan Mawlāy ʿAbd al-Raḥmān withdrew his forces. Despite withdrawing its troops, Morocco would continue to help Algeria throughout the battle. In 1844, Morocco would even offer sanctuary for Algeria's leader, Abdelkader. After offering refuge to Algeria's leader, that same year, Morocco sent military forces to defend the border of Algeria and Morocco, as the French forces were getting close to Morocco's territory.

Despite sending troops to defend the border, on August 4th, 1844, France invaded Tangier, and ten days later, it managed to defeat the entire army stationed at the border city of Isly. On August 15th, it bombarded Essaouira. Realizing the consequences of offering sanctuary to Algeria's leader, Morocco decided to exile Abdelkader. Over the course of the subsequent years, France would continue to invade and attack Algeria. In 1864, Abdelkader would once again attempt to seek refuge in the neighboring country of Morocco; however, this time, Morocco's sultan was not as sympathetic. The Moroccan troops promptly captured Abdelkader and returned him to the French troops, which ultimately forced him to surrender whatever was left of Algeria to the French.

As Morocco passed through the hands of various sultans, it slowly started to lose power. Although Morocco had one of the more advanced armies, as the years went on, it failed to modernize its weapons, techniques, and equipment. Gradually, the various sultans began to lose territory, and as surrounding regions attacked and Europe attempted to colonize Africa, Morocco strained to keep its independence. Over the course of the later years of the 19th century, Morocco's territory was slowly divided. And in 1894, France officially conquered and seized Timbuktu.

Chapter 10 – Timbuktu in the 20th and 21st Centuries (1900–2021)

The Colonization of Morocco

After many conferences between the European forces, it was decided that Morocco was to remain in the hands of the Moroccan government. That being said, France and Spain would be allowed to collect taxes on exports and place policing forces at the ports. Despite the sultan of Morocco at this time being rather content with the outcome of the European conferences, this same attitude was not shared by his family, the nobles, or most of the population, who felt the sultan was getting too close to the Europeans and adapting too many Western ideas.

Throughout the early 20th century, Morocco would wage many rebellions against the European occupation, none of which were actually ordered by the sultan himself. After the sultan was replaced by his brother, who had ordered many of the rebellions and attacks on the Europeans, Morocco struggled to maintain control. Before long, the newly appointed sultan had to sign the Treaty of Fez in 1912, which officially made Morocco a French protectorate. France would end up colonizing most of West Africa, including not only Morocco but also what was once the Mali and Songhai Empires.

As for Timbuktu, while under French control, the city only continued to diminish. While France would invest some funds into restoring the once-great city, the renovations went unfinished. So, even though it was still inhabited, Timbuktu resembled ancient ruins rather than an inhabited city.

French West Africa

Although Timbuktu was a part of Morocco at the time of France's acquisition, it is today a part of modern-day Mali, so it is important to visit the history of Mali to understand what happened to Timbuktu. The Mali of today was added into the mass of territories known as French West Africa, and although the borders would change many times, modern-day Mali was known as French Sudan throughout the 20th century.

French Sudan (modern-day Mali) was colonized and expanded, as France and other European forces were able to conquer nomadic groups surrounding their colonies and trade amongst each other for additional land. At the start of the 20th century, France had commissioned a railroad throughout French West Africa, which helped the colony grow its economy somewhat. Bamako was named French Sudan's capital city, and it remains the capital of Mali today.

France would mainly use its territory in French West Africa to acquire resources, as the land in West Africa was littered with profitable industries, as was obvious with the successful economies of the Mali and Songhai Empires. During World War I, France recruited soldiers from their territories in French West Africa, especially in French Sudan. This was also the case during World War II. However, those who returned home to French Sudan after the Second World War began to gain admiration from other civilians, thus acquiring a small following and power.

Despite drafting many soldiers from Mali, France paid little attention to French Sudan other than to take advantage of some of its income-generating resources. France instead spent far more time and money in Senegal and Cote d'Ivoire (Ivory Coast). This gave the citizens of French Sudan the space to engage in various rebellions and revolts, none of which were successful in even slightly overwhelming France.

Just after the end of World War II, French Sudan began forming its own political parties. While there were many parties, the Sudanese Union-African Democratic Party led by Modibo Keita became a favorite. In 1958, French Sudan changed its name to the Sudanese Republic, and by November 24th of that same year, it joined the French Community and became an autonomous state. The French Community was an attempt by France to hold onto their African colonies while still giving them an amount of autonomy.

Finally, in January of 1959, the Sudanese Republic joined with Senegal to form the Mali Federation, gaining its independence from France and hoping to invite other former French African colonies to join the newly formed federation. Modibo Keita, who had spent years working his way up the ladder of politics and even served as a deputy in the French National Assembly, was chosen as the Mali Federation's first president, despite his strong Marxist opinions.

The First Years of the Republic of Mali

Although the intentions of the Mali Federation were good, no other colonies joined it. Therefore, it essentially became an alliance between two very different countries. It did not take long for Senegal to leave the federation, and the remaining territory and government renamed itself the Republic of Mali.

Promptly after gaining independence from France and separating from Senegal, Modibo Keita began forging a new identity for the Republic of Mali. First, Modibo Keita fired all of the remaining

French governors and civil servants, replacing them with Africans. The first president of the Mali Republic remained true to his Marxist beliefs, issuing a variety of socialist policies, including establishing a state-run economy, issuing its own currency, and forming alliances with other communist countries. Despite all of Modibo Keita's attempts to forge an economy from the ground up, Mali struggled financially, and eventually, he had to request financial aid from France. This communication with Mali's former overlord led to many of his people being against him. On November 19th, 1968, Keita was overthrown in a coup led by Moussa Traoré, who would become the new leader of the republic.

As for Timbuktu, it was acquired by the newly formed Republic of Mali in 1960, but its isolation kept it from experiencing as much change as the rest of the republic. Most of the population was excited about their newly acquired freedom since the nation had gained its independence from France; however, this was not the case for everyone. The Tuareg people who were still living in the Republic of Mali, both in and outside of Timbuktu, did not want to be under another non-Tuareg leader. They decided to once again revolt in an attempt to form their own independent state. Although the Tuaregs had succeeded in gaining independence before, the Republic of Mali's army would prove to be too strong a threat for the rebel Tuaregs. Many of the Tuareg people remaining in Timbuktu and other parts of the Republic of Mali decided to give up and flee to other countries altogether.

The Mali Republic under Traoré's rule

After the coup that brought down Modibo Keita, it would take the Malians a while to stabilize their population and government and return to civilian rule. Part of this was achieved by introducing a new constitution in 1974. In 1979, the Democratic Union of the Malian People was elected, with Moussa Traoré, the man responsible for the coup, as their leader. Although there was an election, the Democratic Union of the Malian People was considered to be the only legal party, and Moussa Traoré and his party would be voted in again in 1985.

Despite his tyrant-like control over the government, Moussa Traoré would prove to be a fair and effective leader, managing to improve the Republic of Mali's situation while putting down internal protests and coups, which happened often. Similar to his predecessor, Moussa Traoré kept positive relationships with communist countries, but he also made an attempt to stay amicable with France. Traoré even went further than any African leader of that region had done before by forging positive relations with the United States. He believed an alliance with them would attract American investments and help to diversify the Republic of Mali's economy.

Meanwhile, as the president of the Republic of Mali attempted to improve foreign affairs, its internal affairs were not the best. The remaining Tuareg people in the republic were still hoping to gain their independence, and by the summer of 1990, the Second Tuareg Rebellion had begun. After nearly five years of warring, the president of Mali decided to give the Tuareg some independence in the Kidal region, which included much of former Gao.

And it was not just the Tuareg people demanding greater independence but the Malian civilians as well. In 1991, riots for democracy were breaking out all over Mali, which led to the imprisonment of Moussa Traoré. The Republic of Mali was then taken over by Amadou Toumani Touré and his military government, who promised to help stabilize the government and return Mali to a democratic society with civilian rule. As promised, democratic elections for the presidency were held in 1992, and Amadou Toumani Touré was elected. Amadou Toumani Touré would be reelected as president in 2002 and 2007, and he would hold the position until 2012.

Amadou Toumani Touré's Terms as President

Despite claiming leadership in a militant way, after being officially voted in as president, Amadou Toumani Touré would take great strides toward peace and actually manage to stabilize a dissatisfied population for a short time. In 2006, he even managed to reach a peace agreement with some of the Tuareg rebels, although the agreement only applied to the Tuaregs in the northern desert of Mali. In other parts of Niger and Mali, more Tuareg rebellions would break out again, starting in 2007. To add insult to injury, Mali was also home to a network of al-Qaeda, and there were wars breaking out both in and against the surrounding countries.

One example of a war in a surrounding country is the Libyan Civil War, which recruited many of Mali's Tuareg people to fight. After the war, Mali's Tuaregs returned home, armed, trained, and prepared to fight for their own independence. The Tuaregs' main goal was to create their own, self-governed state, which they planned to call Azawad. In some northern towns, the Tuareg people even managed to take over, resulting in most of the non-Tuareg population fleeing for safety.

Although Amadou Toumani Touré had managed to achieve peace early in his presidency, by 2012, Mali was no longer peaceful, and the population was no longer satisfied with his leadership. Just as Amadou Toumani Touré had claimed power in a military coup years before, power was taken away from him on March 21st, 2012, in a military coup led by the National Committee for the Recovery of Democracy and Restoration of the State, which was led by Amadou Haya Sanogo.

As Malians and surrounding countries tried to figure out what to do with the administration of the Republic of Mali, the Tuareg people, who became known as the National Movement for the Liberation of Azawad (MNLA), formed an alliance with an Islamist group, Ansar Dine (Defenders of the Faith). Although the alliance would break through, the short-lived partnership allowed Ansar Dine to take control of some of the Republic of Mali, including the city of Timbuktu. Unlike the Tuaregs, who simply wanted their own state, Ansar Dine wanted to take over the entire Republic of Mali and enforce strict Sharia law.

As tensions rose, more terrorist groups created bases in Mali, which, of course, posed another threat to democracy. At the end of 2012, the situation in Mali had become so bad that the Tuareg or MNLA, Ansar Dine, and the Republic of Mali's government met and agreed to a ceasefire, as well as another meeting to discuss the future of Mali. However, before peace could ever really be enjoyed, the warring started up again. In order to prevent a massive civil war, a United Nations-backed support, known as the African-led International Support Mission (AFISMA), was called into Mali.

But before any foreign aid could arrive, the situation in Mali got worse, as more land was captured by extremist Islamic groups. By January of 2013, troops from AFISMA and France, in addition to those of the Republic of Mali, were fighting Islamist forces and reclaiming territory. By April, the Republic of Mali had regained all of its territories, including the city of Timbuktu. To ensure that it would remain secure, the United Nations Security Council created the Multidimensional Integrated Stabilization Mission in Mali (MINUSMA). In the summer of 2013, a peace accord was drawn up and signed by both the Mali government and the Tuareg people. Finally, after an insane year of warring, Mali attempted to return to its previous democratic self by hosting official elections on July 28th, 2013. Ibrahim Boubacar Keita was officially voted in.

Although there were democratic elections at last, the Republic of Mali had not seen the end of violence, both with internal groups and external countries. In 2018, Ibrahim Boubacar Keita was reelected, yet the issues of violence only intensified. This led to not only a crumbling economy but also a dissatisfied population.

Although Keita's presidency was still continuing in 2020, his term came to an early end, as a military government known as the Salvation of the People (CNSP) arrested him and forced him to resign. This was a controversial move, and it was worrisome to everyone but the Malians who appreciated the change of government. A new civil election is set to take place in February of 2022.

After all of the warring in Mali's more recent history, Timbuktu had been mostly destroyed, although some structures, art, and manuscripts were protected and remain intact. The city, which is now considered to be a UNESCO World Heritage Site, is undergoing renovations in order to repair some of the damage of the past few decades.

Conclusion

Although Timbuktu is considered to be a UNESCO World Heritage site, it is on the verge of being destroyed at any moment due to the ongoing wars in the Republic of Mali. The once-great Timbuktu is again in danger of collapse, as violent groups plague the city and its surrounding areas. Even though the globe has become more connected than ever before, Timbuktu has remained in the past. With no easy transit routes, the city receives few tourists and even fewer settlers who would want to live in Timbuktu, especially considering the dangerous battles occurring around it.

The Republic of Mali's future is hard enough to predict. However, it is even harder to predict the future of the isolated city of Timbuktu, especially considering it has been contested since the 11th century. Although this isn't the first time Timbuktu has been destroyed and rebuilt, then turned to ruins and returned to glory, it doesn't seem like any solution is working in Timbuktu, particularly since terrorist forces have taken over the city.

Timbuktu once had a reputation of containing so much gold that Europeans lost their lives trying to locate it. People traversed the brutal Sahara Desert just to reach it. Now, the city, which was once the epicenter of Muslim education, is the home to Al-Qaeda and other terrorist groups. The only travelers are those who have to visit, such as workers from the United Nations, military troops, and journalists. The population of Timbuktu is now only fifteen thousand, making it ten thousand less than the number of students who were estimated to have attended the University of Sankoré during the city's peak years.

Although Timbuktu and the Mali Empire were once the centers for agriculture, the canals have dried up, and nowadays, the people struggle to grow enough for themselves, let alone to sell. Most of the remaining Tuareg have either been killed, been colonized, or left Timbuktu and Mali altogether. The most likely outcome for Timbuktu is that the rest of the population follow the example of the Tuareg and leave the city for good, as they will end up assimilating or die trying to reclaim it from its violent leaders. However, with the various powers fighting terrorism, there is always a chance for the city to be restored and cleansed of its violent parties.

Regardless of the future of the city, most of Timbuktu's sacred items are being exported, as people fear their destruction. Books from the reign of Mansa Musa I have been collected, as well as the incredible art that was created. It is hopeful that everything with historical value, short of the iconic structures themselves, will gradually be removed from the dangerous city.

All in all, the city of Timbuktu helped shape the world in so many ways, and although its future is uncertain, its past influence is not debatable. While mythical-sounding stories of its glory matched with its current isolation and terrorist dangers have made many people doubt its existence, Timbuktu is real. It was once a glorious city that may cease to exist any day.

Here's another book by Captivating History that you might like

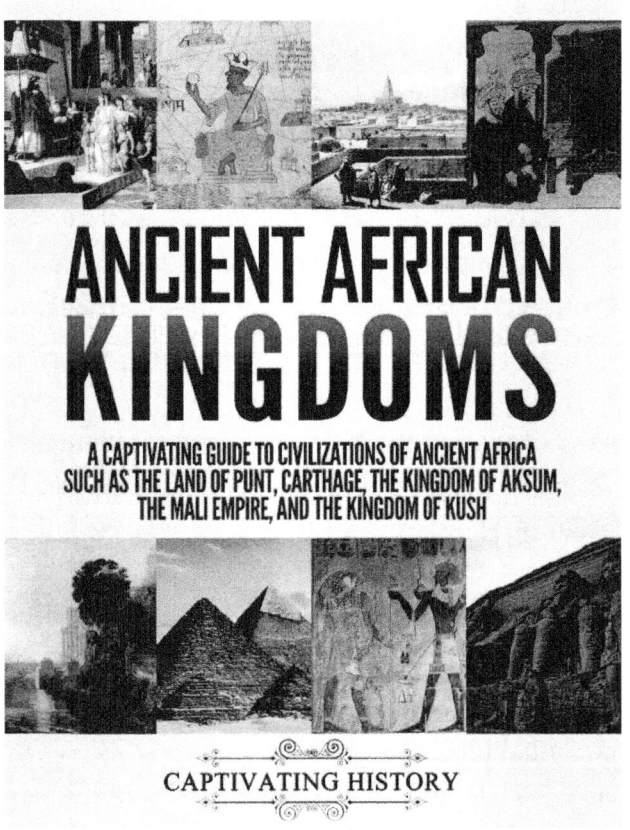

Free Bonus from Captivating History (Available for a Limited time)

Hi History Lovers!

Now you have a chance to join our exclusive history list so you can get your first history ebook for free as well as discounts and a potential to get more history books for free! Simply visit the link below to join.

Captivatinghistory.com/ebook

Also, make sure to follow us on Facebook, Twitter and Youtube by searching for Captivating History.

Bibliography

Mansa Musa: The Most Famous African Traveler to Mecca. Barbara Krasner. 2016.

Mansa Musa I: Kankan Moussa from Niani to Mecca. Jean-Louis Roy. 2019.

Mansa Musa and Timbuktu. Charles River Editors. 2019.

Mansa Musa: Leader of Mali. Lisa Zamosky. 2007.

When Sundiata Keita Built the Mali Empire. Baby Professor. 2017.

Empires of Medieval West Africa. David C. Conrad. 2009.

The Adventures of Ibn Battuta: A Muslim Traveler of the 14th Century. Ross E. Dunn. 2012.

Mansa Musa and the Empire of Mali: A True Story of Gold and Greatness from Africa. James P. Oliver. 2013.

Encyclopedia of African History: Volume 1 A-G. Kevin Shillington. 2005.

The Quran. (Translated by M. H. Shakir). 1993.

23andMe. "People of the Veil: New Study Reveals Clues to Origins of the Nomadic Tuaregs." *23andMe Blog*, 2 June 2009, https://blog.23andme.com/23andme-and-you/genetics-101/people-of-the-veil-new-study-reveals-clues-to-origins-of-the-nomadic-tuaregs

Academic Dictionaries and Encyclopedias. "Kassa (Mansa)." *Academic Dictionaries and Encyclopedias*, 2021, https://en-academic.com/dic.nsf/enwiki/1075753

Academic Dictionaries and Encyclopedias. "Uli I of Mali." *Academic Dictionaries and Encyclopedias*, 2021, https://en-academic.com/dic.nsf/enwiki/11688752

BBC News. "BBC World Service | the Story of Africa." *BBC News*, BBC, 2021, https://www.bbc.co.uk/worldservice/specials/1624_story_of_africa/page82.shtml

Bradshaw Foundation. "The Tuareg the Nomadic Inhabitants of North Africa." *Bradshaw Foundation*, 2021, https://www.bradshawfoundation.com/tuareg/index.php

Britannica, The Editors of Encyclopedia. "Aḥmad Bābā." *Encyclopedia Britannica*, Encyclopedia Britannica, Inc., 2021, https://www.britannica.com/biography/Ahmad-Baba

Britannica, The Editors of Encyclopedia. "Djenné." *Encyclopedia Britannica*, Encyclopedia Britannica, Inc., 13 Jan. 2020, https://www.britannica.com/place/Djenne

Britannica, The Editors of Encyclopedia. "Gao." *Encyclopedia Britannica*, Encyclopedia Britannica, Inc., 12 Feb. 2013, https://www.britannica.com/place/Gao-Mali

Britannica, The Editors of Encyclopedia. "Mali." *Encyclopedia Britannica*, Encyclopedia Britannica, Inc., 5 Sept. 2021, https://www.britannica.com/place/Mali-historical-empire-Africa

Britannica, The Editors of Encyclopedia. "Malinke." *Encyclopedia Britannica*, Encyclopedia Britannica, Inc., 10 Dec. 2017, https://www.britannica.com/topic/Malinke

Britannica, The Editors of Encyclopedia. "Songhai Empire." *Encyclopedia Britannica*, Encyclopedia Britannica, Inc., 25 Apr. 2021, https://www.britannica.com/place/Songhai-empire

Britannica, The Editors of Encyclopedia. "Sumanguru." *Encyclopedia Britannica*, Encyclopedia Britannica, Inc., 28 Jan. 2015, https://www.britannica.com/biography/Sumanguru

Britannica, The Editors of Encyclopedia. "Sumanguru." *Encyclopedia Britannica*, Encyclopedia Britannica, Inc., 28 Jan. 2015, https://www.britannica.com/biography/Sumanguru

Britannica, The Editors of Encyclopedia. "Sumanguru." *Encyclopedia Britannica*, Encyclopedia Britannica, Inc., 28 Jan. 2015, https://www.britannica.com/biography/Sumanguru

Britannica, The Editors of Encyclopedia. "Sundiata Keita." *Encyclopedia Britannica*, Encyclopedia Britannica, Inc., 21 Jan. 2021, https://www.britannica.com/biography/Sundiata-Keita

Britannica, The Editors of Encyclopedia. "Timbuktu." *Encyclopedia Britannica*, Encyclopedia Britannica, Inc., 25 Nov. 2019, https://www.britannica.com/place/Timbuktu-Mali

Britannica, The Editors of Encyclopedia. "Tuareg." *Encyclopedia Britannica*, Encyclopedia Britannica, Inc., 20 Mar. 2019, https://www.britannica.com/topic/Tuareg

Cartwright, Mark. "Timbuktu." *World History Encyclopedia*, World History Encyclopedia, 22 Feb. 2019, https://www.worldhistory.org/Timbuktu

Ducksters. "Biography: Sundiata Keita of Mali." *Ducksters*, Technological Solutions, Inc. (TSI), 2021, https://www.ducksters.com/history/africa/sundiata_keita.php

Geoghegan, Tom. "Who, What, Why: Why Do We Know Timbuktu?" *BBC News*, BBC, 2 Apr. 2012, https://www.bbc.com/news/magazine-17583772

Graft-Johnson, John Coleman de. "Mūsā I of Mali." *Encyclopedia Britannica*, Encyclopedia Britannica, Inc., 3 Feb. 2021, https://www.britannica.com/biography/Musa-I-of-Mali

Hammer, Joshua. "The Treasures of Timbuktu." *Smithsonian.com*, Smithsonian Institution, 1 Dec. 2006, https://www.smithsonianmag.com/history/the-treasures-of-timbuktu-138566090

HRF. "10 Major Accomplishments of Mansa Musa." *HealthResearchFunding.org*, 2021, https://healthresearchfunding.org/10-major-accomplishments-of-mansa-musa

Jackson, Kellie Carter. "Perspective | the True Story behind 'the Lion King'." *The Washington Post*, WP Company, 17 July 2019, https://www.washingtonpost.com/outlook/2019/07/17/true-story-behind-lion-king

Jarus, Owen. "Timbuktu: History of Fabled Center of Learning." *LiveScience*, Purch, 21 Jan. 2013, https://www.livescience.com/26451-timbuktu.html

Keys, David. "Mali: The History behind the World's Newest Conflict." *Aspenia Online*, Aspenia Online, 2013, https://www.aspeniaonline.it/wp-content/uploads/2013/04/keys-ing_080413.pdf

Lawton, Bishop. "Sankore Mosque and University." *Sankore Mosque and University*, 20 Jan. 2021, https://www.blackpast.org/global-african-history/institutions-global-african-history/sankore-mosque-and-university-c-1100

Levtzion, N., "The Thirteenth- and Fourteenth-Century Kings of Mali." *The Journal of African History*, vol. 4, no. 3, 1963, https://www.jstor.org/stable/180027. Accessed Sept. 2021

Lumencandela. "West African Empires." *Lumen Boundless World History*, 2021, https://courses.lumenlearning.com/boundless-worldhistory/chapter/west-african-empires

Mohamud, Naima. "Is Mansa Musa the Richest Man Who Ever Lived?" *BBC News*, BBC, 10 Mar. 2019, https://www.bbc.com/news/world-africa-47379458

Morgan, Thad. "This 14th-Century African Emperor Remains the Richest Person in History." *History.com*, A&E Television Networks, 19 Mar. 2018, https://www.history.com/news/who-was-the-richest-man-in-history-mansa-musa

National Geographic Society. "Mansa Musa (Musa I of Mali)." *National Geographic Society*, 14 Apr. 2020, https://www.nationalgeographic.org/encyclopedia/mansa-musa-musa-i-mali

National Geographic Society. "The Mali Empire." *National Geographic Society*, 19 Aug. 2020, https://www.nationalgeographic.org/encyclopedia/mali-empire

Nduneseokwu, Chuka. "Battle of Kirina – the Battle That Gave Rise to the African Mali Empire." *Liberty Writers Global*, 17 Dec. 2020, https://libertywritersglobal.com/battle-of-kirina-the-battle-that-gave-rise-to-the-african-mali-empire

Nelson, Kieron. "Tuaregs: 'Abandoned by God.'" *Vanishing Cultures Photography*, 1999, https://www.vanishingculturesphotography.com/p453343259/h146B7522

Neuman, Scott. "From Here to Timbuktu: Myth and Reality at the World's Edge." *National Public Radio*, NPR, 29 Jan. 2013, https://www.npr.org/2013/01/29/170562921/from-here-to-timbuktu-myth-and-reality-at-the-world-s-edge

New World Encyclopedia. "Berber." *Berber - New World Encyclopedia*, 2016, https://www.newworldencyclopedia.org/entry/Berber

New World Encyclopedia. "Mali Empire." *Mali Empire - New World Encyclopedia*, 18 Aug. 2018, https://www.newworldencyclopedia.org/entry/Mali_Empire

New World Encyclopedia. "Tuareg." *Tuareg - New World Encyclopedia*, 27 Mar. 2020, https://www.newworldencyclopedia.org/entry/tuareg

O'Neill, Aaron. "Population of the Continents 10,000BCE-2000CE." *Statista*, Statista Research Department, 31 Dec. 2007, https://www.statista.com/statistics/1006557/global-population-per-continent-10000bce-2000ce

Schools Wikipedia Selection. *Timbuktu*. McGill University, 2007, https://www.cs.mcgill.ca/~rwest/wikispeedia/wpcd/wp/t/Timbuktu.htm

Smith, Alex Duval. "Life in Timbuktu: How the Ancient City of Gold Is Slowly Turning to Dust." *The Guardian*, Guardian News and Media, 16 Sept. 2014, https://www.theguardian.com/cities/2014/sep/16/-sp-life-timbuktu-mali-ancient-city-gold-slowly-turning-to-dust

Smith, Jessica, and Sandro Katamashvili. *Mansa Musa, One of the Wealthiest People Who Ever Lived*. YouTube, Ted-Ed, 18 May 2015, https://www.youtube.com/watch?v=O3YJMaL55TM&ab_channel=TED-Ed. Accessed Sept. 2021

Swearingen, Will D., Brown, L. Carl, Miller, Susan Gilson, Barbour, Nevill and Laroui, Abdallah. "Morocco." *Encyclopedia Britannica*, Encyclopedia Britannica, Inc., 17 Sept. 2021, https://www.britannica.com/place/Morocco

Tesfu, Julianna. "Timbuktu (Ca. 1100-)." *Blackpast.org*, 29 June 2008, https://www.blackpast.org/global-african-history/timbuktu-ca-1100

UNESCO World Heritage Centre. "Timbuktu." *UNESCO World Heritage Centre*, 2021, https://whc.unesco.org/en/list/119

Virginia Department of Education. "MALI: ANCIENT CROSSROADS OF AFRICA: HISTORY." *VDOE*, Commonwealth of Virginia, 2021, https://www.doe.virginia.gov/instruction/history/mali/history/index.shtml

Printed in Great Britain
by Amazon